Edinburgh Law Essentials

SCOTTISH FAMILY LAW

D1427253

EDINBURGH LAW ESSENTIALS

Series Editor: Nicholas Grier, Edinburgh Napier University

Private International Law
David Hill

Revenue Law Essentials
William Craig

Commercial Law Essentials
Malcolm Combe

Succession Law Essentials
Frankie McCarthy

Delict Essentials
Francis McManus

Scottish Legal System Essentials
Bryan Clark and Gerard Keegan

Evidence Essentials
James Chalmers

Contract Law Essential Cases
Tikus Little

Trusts Law Essentials
John Finlay

Company Law Essentials
Josephine Bisacre and Claire McFadzean

Jurisprudence Essentials
Duncan Spiers

Legal Method Essentials
Dale McFadzean and Gareth Ryan

Human Rights Law Essentials
Valerie Finch and John McGroarty

Planning Law Essentials
Anne-Michelle Slater

Scottish Contract Law
Tikus Little

Employment Law Essentials
Jenifer Ross

International Law Essentials
John Grant

Media Law Essentials
Douglas Maule and Zhongdong Niu

Intellectual Property Law Essentials
Duncan Spiers

Scottish Family Law
Kenneth Norrie

European Law Essentials
Stephanie Switzer

Roman Law Essentials
Craig Anderson

Property Law Essentials
Duncan Spiers

Medical Law Essentials
Murray Earle

Public Law Essentials
Jean McFadden and Dale McFadzean

Scottish Administrative Law Essentials
Jean McFadden and Dale McFadzean

www.euppublishing.com/series/ele

Edinburgh Law Essentials

SCOTTISH FAMILY LAW

Third edition

Kenneth McK. Norrie

Professor of Law,
University of Strathclyde

EDINBURGH
University Press

© Kenneth McK. Norrie, 2015

First edition published in 2006 by Dundee University Press
Second edition 2009

Edinburgh University Press Ltd
The Tun – Holyrood Road
12 (2f) Jackson's Entry
Edinburgh EH8 8PJ
www.euppublishing.com

Typeset in Bembo by
3btype.com and
printed and bound in Great Britain by
CPI Group (UK) Ltd, Croydon CR0 4YY

A CIP record for this book is available from the British Library

ISBN 978 1 4744 0339 9 (hardback)
ISBN 978 1 84586 153 7 (paperback)
ISBN 978 1 4744 0198 2 (webready PDF)
ISBN 978 1 4744 0199 9 (epub)

CONTENTS

PREFACE

Family law is the system of rules and regulations that govern the creation of families and regulate the relationships both between family members and between such members and the rest of the world. These rules reflect the society that they serve and, as Scottish society changes, so does Scottish family law. The subject is normally split into two major elements: the parent–child relationship and the adult–adult relationship, though today the one is far less dependent on the other than it was in the past. Both relationships exist outwith the bounds of a legal system, but the law defines and controls, more or less artificially, both forms of relationship by a matrix of interconnected rules. The parent–child relationship, as we will see, is affected by the status of the parent and can be recognised legally even in the absence of a scientifically defined (genetic, or blood) relationship. Adult–adult relationships are typified but not today limited to marriage – not only was a new and equivalent institution, civil partnership, a twenty-first-century creation for same-sex couples, introduced before the ancient and venerable institution of marriage itself was opened to these couples, but more informal relationships based simply on the fact of the couple living together are now recognised and controlled (while not created) by law. This short book is designed to give the broad outlines of the legal controls of families, both formally and informally constituted, that exist in Scotland. The law is as stated on 16 December 2014.

HOW TO USE THIS BOOK

This book is written to provide a skeleton guide for students studying Scottish family law, with the aim of making the various statutes, cases and common law rules as readily accessible as possible. Each chapter contains a narrative text, followed by a list of the essential facts that must be learnt by anyone wishing to understand the subject, a list of the essential statutory provisions that make up the bulk of Scottish family law and a list of the essential cases that illustrate or develop these facts and show how the statutes operate in practice. Each chapter should be read as a whole, and as a part of the whole book. There are no footnotes, and only minimal statutory references in the narrative itself.

Students should, however, be careful in how they use this book. It should not be used instead of more substantial textbooks; far less should it be used to replace lecture notes taken in class. It does not give full details, nor complete references, nor comprehensive explanations of the principles behind the rules. You will not pass your exams at any Scottish Law School simply by memorising the facts, cases and statutes described in this book. The cases can, of course, only be properly understood by reading the judgments themselves; the statutes can only be properly understood by understanding the political debates behind them. This book should be regarded more as a road map than a definitive text, for various propositions set out in the pages that follow are in reality subject to conditions and qualifications that we do not have the time or space to go into. Historical context is, of necessity, almost completely absent. The book is a brief introduction to, and not a definitive exposition of, contemporary Scottish family law but it is hoped that this road map will make the navigation through the statutes, cases and other textbooks rather easier by students coming to the subject for the first time. Depth of understanding will be acquired elsewhere, but it is hoped that this book will allow that understanding to be acquired more readily. It is hoped, also, that the book will show just how very interesting the law of family relationships actually is.

TABLE OF CASES

TABLE OF STATUTES

1 LEGAL PERSONALITY

Family law is primarily the law of natural persons and, as such, a number of issues need to be examined before moving on to the major part of the discipline, which is how the law regulates personal relationships between natural persons. The concept of natural person requires us to examine (i) the nature and acquisition of legal personality; (ii) age; and (iii) gender.

NATURE AND ACQUISITION OF LEGAL PERSONALITY

Legal personality is the concept whereby a "person" is recognised as existing by the law in a juridically active sense: in other words as an entity that can perform juridical acts such as entering into contracts, suing and being sued, and owning and dealing with property. Without legal personality an entity can be no more than the subject of legal rights and responsibilities – it cannot be the holder thereof. A building, an animal or a tree has no legal personality and so cannot own property, enter contracts, marry or be sued. A limited liability company or other incorporated body, on the other hand, does have legal personality and so can be the holder of legal rights and responsibilities; and so too, in a system that eschews slavery, will every natural human person. Legal personality in this sense is acquired by natural persons at the moment of live birth. Before then, while there exists an entity that might be entitled to legal protection, that entity is not entitled to own property, to sue or be sued, or to enter into contracts.

So the child before birth has no legal personality, but this is not to deny that anything exists or is recognised by the law: it merely denies the child's power to own property and so on. The law of abortion, for example, recognises the existence of the child before birth and provides protection from unlawful abortion, but that is very different from saying the child before birth has legal personality. Rather, an unborn child is like a listed building: it exists in the physical world and is protected by the law to the extent that before it can be destroyed various permissions are demanded. The present law of abortion in Scotland is a mixture of common law and statute. The common law prohibits it as a crime, and statute (the Abortion Act 1967, as amended by the Human Fertilisation and Embryology Act 1990) provides a potential accused with various defences to the criminal charge. These are as follows:

(1) that the continuation of the pregnancy would involve risk, greater than if the pregnancy were terminated, of injury to the physical or mental health of the pregnant woman or any existing children of her family (this ground being available only during the first twenty-four weeks of pregnancy);

(2) that the termination is necessary to prevent grave permanent injury to the physical or mental health of the pregnant woman (no time limit);

(3) that the continuation of the pregnancy would involve risk to the life of the pregnant woman, greater than if the pregnancy were terminated (no time limit);

(4) that there is a substantial risk that if the child were born it would suffer from such physical or mental abnormalities as to be seriously handicapped (no time limit).

However, it should be noted that these defences need exist only in the mind of the accused, and *not* in fact. So a prosecutor must show (and remember that as a criminal charge it must be shown beyond reasonable doubt) that the accused did not believe in good faith that any of the above circumstances existed. It is nothing to the point whether or not, for example, the woman's life was really at any risk.

The child before birth is also entitled to be protected from harm short of destruction, and the source of this harm is often the mother. It is not, however, possible to take action against the mother (such as locking her up) to prevent her from, for example, taking drugs that will harm her child. But the behaviour of a pregnant woman during pregnancy can be used to justify removing the child after it is born if this behaviour indicates a likelihood that the woman or her lifestyle will continue to harm the child after birth.

The child before birth is recognised as existing for other purposes even without the attribution of legal personality. It was accepted in Roman law and remains the case in Scots law today that a posthumous child is entitled to succession rights. So if, for example, a father dies before his child is born, that child will be entitled to claim a share of his estate. This is known as the *nasciturus* principle. Its application is, however, subject to two conditions: first, the claim must be to a direct benefit and not indirect, for example traced through another person, and, second, the child must be subsequently born alive. Another requirement, flowing from s 41(2) of the Human Fertilisation and Embryology Act 2008, is that the embryo that grows into the child must begin so to grow during the life of the father. The statute uses the less than obvious language of the father's sperm, or the embryo created with his sperm, being "used" before his death, but the meaning is fairly clear. If a man's sperm is used to create an embryo during his life, or if the embryo so created is implanted into a woman during his life, then any subsequent child that results from this is in law his and succession rights arise, but if the child is created with his sperm used for that purpose after his death he is not the father for purposes of succession, or virtually any other purpose of law. The only exception is that he will be treated as the father for the purpose of being registered as such in the Register of Births (2008 Act, s 40), but this has no practical consequence in law.

AGE

A person's age is crucial to the law for that person's status, and age is counted from the beginning of the day upon which the person is born. So a person becomes 16 at the beginning of the 16th anniversary of his or her birth (Age of Legal Capacity (Scotland) Act 1991, s 6). There is in Scotland no single age at which a person moves from childhood to adulthood. Rather, it depends entirely upon the issue, and the so-called 'age of majority' (which is 18) is virtually limited in terms of legal consequence to the age of voting – and even that is no longer as absolute as it once was. Twelve is the crucial age for making a will and consenting to adoption; 16 is the age of marriage/civil partnership, lawful "sexual activity" within the terms of the Sexual Offences (Scotland) Act 2009, and the escaping from parental rights; 18 is the age at which young persons can vote in UK parliamentary elections (though the 2014 Scottish independence referendum permitted 16 and 17 year olds to vote). There are various other statutory ages dealing with matters such as driving a car, joining the army, being employed, leaving school and so on. Additionally, there are certain juridical activities at which no specified age is laid down for everyone: instead, the law treats each individual separately and determines on a case-by-case basis whether the young person is old enough to do this or that. Entering into legal transactions (typically contracts) is the most important example, and the Age of Legal Capacity (Scotland) Act 1991, s 2(1) provides that a person under the age of 16 can do this so long as (i) the transaction is of a type that is not uncommon in that person's age and circumstances and (ii) its terms and conditions are not unreasonable. Another example is giving consent to medical treatment, which can be done by a person under the age of 16 so long as he or she understands (in the view of the health care professional providing the treatment) the nature and possible consequences of the treatment (1991 Act, s 2(4)). Likewise a child under 16 can instruct a solicitor and raise or defend civil proceedings in a court of law so long as he or she understands what it means to do so (1991 Act, s 2(4A) and (4B)). Children who do not have capacity for any of these acts will need to have them carried out on their behalf by their "legal representatives".

The parental responsibility and right of legal representation terminates when the child reaches the age of 16, from which point the young person must act on his or her own behalf. The law continues to provide some protection, however, and any transaction entered into before the young person reaches the age of 18 can be reduced (that is to say, nullified) if it can be shown to be a transaction that (i) an adult, exercising reasonable prudence, would not have entered into in the young person's circumstances and (ii) has caused or is likely to cause substantial prejudice to the young person. Both conditions must be satisfied if the transaction is to be reduced, and the young person must seek to have it reduced before his or her 21st birthday. Section 3(3) of the 1991 Act lists the transactions that are not open to reduction on the ground of substantial prejudice, such as making a will, bringing or defending civil legal proceedings, and transactions in the course of the young person's trade, business or profession.

GENDER

Modern society continues to be gendered both socially and legally. Socially we continue to expect individuals' places and roles to be determined by their gender; legally the law still requires certain activities to be carried out by one gender rather than the other. Within family law the institution of civil partnership remains gendered in that it can be contracted only by two persons who are of the same sex as each other and even although marriage can be either opposite-sex or same-sex, marriage is not gender-neutral since celebrants need to be explicitly authorised to perform ceremonies for opposite-sex couples, for same-sex couples or for both. So how does the law define whether a person is male or female?

For most people this is a matter that is both obvious and unambiguous. For at least two categories, however, the issue raises serious doubts. First, there are individuals who are born with mixed gender characteristics: the so-called intersex persons. There are a variety of medical syndromes and chromosomal abnormalities which lead to individuals possessing characteristics of both sexes. Though there has been little discussion of the matter in Scotland, such authority as we have suggests that a "predominance" approach is taken to classify such individuals as either "male" or "female". By this is meant that the various factors that normally all point in the same direction (chromosomes, hormones, gonads, genitalia, self-perception, social role) are weighted and the person is deemed male or female by whichever is predominant. And if a mistake is made at birth and the child is registered as the wrong gender because, for example, only external appearance was taken into account, then this can be corrected later.

Second, there are individuals whose physical characteristics, both external and internal, are clearly of one gender but their brain tells them irresistibly that they are of the other gender. Such people are called transsexuals, transgender people or trans people. For many decades now it has been possible to ameliorate the immense distress this disjunction of body and mind causes by hormonal and surgical treatment designed to make such individuals' bodies look more like the gender their mind tells them they belong to. But the law was for a long time rigid in defining a person's gender as that which was physically (externally) presented at birth. Put simply, "sex change" was not legally possible.

However, this position was reversed after the European Court of Human Rights held it to be incompatible with the European Convention on Human Rights, as a breach of both Art 8 (right to private life) and Art 12 (right to marry). The UK Government responded with the Gender Recognition Act 2004 which set up a Gender Recognition Panel. This Panel, on the basis of evidence presented before it, is able to determine that an applicant who used to be of one gender is now of the opposite gender. If this determination is made then the Panel will grant a "gender recognition certificate", which amounts to a change of the legal sex of the applicant for virtually all purposes of law including, crucially, marriage and civil partnership. (Exceptions include for sporting competitions and gender-specific crimes; and a trans person will retain his or her previous status as "father" or "mother" of any child.) A married person who seeks a gender recognition certificate will, however, be granted only an interim gender recognition certificate, which provides a ground for divorce. But often the couple wish to stay together and so if the trans person's spouse consents to remaining married the Gender Recognition Panel can grant a full gender recognition certificate; if the spouse does not consent the sheriff will grant a full gender recognition certificate after an interim certificate has been granted by the Panel, and the spouse can protect his or her own interests by using that interim certificate to obtain a divorce.

Essential Facts

- Legal personality begins at the moment of live birth.
- Abortion is a crime but medical practitioners have various defences.
- An unborn child will be treated as being in life whenever this is to its direct advantage.
- A child created through the use of a dead man's sperm has no legal father.
- A person's gender is initially determined by biological criteria, though it can be lawfully changed by the acquisition of a gender recognition certificate granted by the Gender Recognition Panel.

Essential Statutes

Abortion Act 1967

Section 1 sets out the defences to the common law crime of abortion. Section 4 provides for a conscientious objection to those who oppose abortion and would otherwise be obliged to participate in any treatment authorised by the 1967 Act.

Age of Legal Capacity (Scotland) Act 1991

Section 1 grants legal capacity to perform transactions that have legal effect to all those who are 16 years of age or older, and withholds such capacity from those younger than 16. Section 2 sets out the exceptions to the under 16 year old's lack of capacity and allows those under 16 to perform various legal acts themselves (subject to different criteria laid down in each specified exception). Section 3 allows the court to set aside transactions entered into by 16 to 18 year olds where the transaction is "prejudicial", as defined.

Gender Recognition Act 2004

Section 1 allows a person over the age of 18 to apply for a gender recognition certificate. Section 2 sets out the conditions which have to be satisfied for the granting of a gender recognition certificate. Section 9 sets out the consequences of obtaining a gender recognition certificate, which is that a person is treated in law as of the gender opposite to that which he or she was treated by the law until then. Sections 12–16 set out the exceptions, including that the person's status of parent in relation to his or her children is unaffected, and that succession to peerages and titles of honour is unaffected.

Essential Cases

Cox's Trs v Cox (1950): Mr Charles Cox was a wealthy solicitor in Banchory. When he died he left his property to the descendants (children, grandchildren and so on) of his four brothers and his sister. Four such descendants were born after Mr Cox's death, but had been *in utero* at the date of death. The court applied the *nasciturus* principle that an unborn child will be treated as born whenever it is to the unborn child's advantage, and so the unborn descendants were entitled to share the legacy.

Elliot v Joicey (1935): a legacy was to be divided amongst certain named children. If any predeceasing child had died childless his or her share was to go to the other named children; if any predeceasing children had died survived by children of their own their share was to remain in their estate (for distribution to their own children). One child predeceased leaving a child *in utero*.

The court held that the *nasciturus* principle, under which a child *in utero* will be treated as being in life, only applied when it was of direct benefit to the unborn child and that in this case the benefit did not directly accrue to the unborn child but to the estate of its parent (the testator's child). So the predeceasing (testator's) child was held to have died childless.

Doogan and Wood v Greater Glasgow and Clyde Health Board (2014): Doogan and Woods were midwives who were employed as labour ward co-ordinators at a Glasgow hospital. That ward contained patients who had undergone abortions and the midwives, who professed the Roman Catholic faith, expressed a conscientious objection to doing their jobs in respect of abortion patients on the ward. The Abortion Act 1967 allows individuals who have a conscientious objection to abortion to refuse to "participate in any treatment" authorised by the 1967 Act. The question for the court was whether acting as ward supervisors in a ward that contained patients undergoing an abortion was "participating in" the treatment (provision of abortion) authorised by the 1967 Act.

Though the judge at first instance held that the ward co-ordinators were not participating in abortion treatment, the Inner House overruled this, holding that any part of the medical care given as a result of abortion is included in the conscientious objection provision. The Inner House was, in turn, overruled by the Supreme Court, which held that "participating in" the treatment meant being involved in a "hands on" capacity: the labour ward co-ordinators lost their claim because their involvement was too removed from the abortion procedure.

The Inner House also held that conscientious objection did not apply to the second defence to abortion, when it is necessary to prevent grave permanent injury to the health of the mother but the Supreme Court did not address this point.

D (A Minor) v Berkshire County Council (1987): a child was born suffering from drug withdrawal symptoms and had been removed from the care of its parents immediately on birth: the ground for removal was that the child "was being harmed" by the parents. The parents argued that since the child had been removed immediately on birth they never had the chance to harm the child.

The court held that the child was being harmed by the mother before birth by her taking of drugs and therefore could be removed from the parents, even before they had been given an opportunity to show whether they would look after the child properly.

M v Scottish Children's Reporter for Renfrewshire (2009): a child was referred to a children's hearing on the ground that he was likely to suffer unnecessarily or be impaired seriously in his health or development due to a lack of parental care. The referral was made shortly after his birth. The basis of concern was the fact that the mother had an earlier child (now in care) and that she had a relationship with a man who had a history of sexually abusing children.

The court held that the risk to the new-born child had been made out: it was legitimate to look at events in the past, such as the mother's failure to protect her earlier child from the attentions of her partner, in order to assess the likelihood of the new-born child suffering unnecessarily while in her care.

Re MB (1997): a woman who was about to give birth to a child was advised that she needed to have a Caesarean section for the good of the child. She refused because she had a needle phobia. The health authority sought a court order permitting it to perform the operation without her consent.

The Court of Appeal held that an adult competent patient had an absolute right to refuse consent to medical treatment, for good reason or bad, or no reason at all. Operations without consent can be performed only when the patient lacks mental competence. In this case the woman's needle phobia took away her power of rational thought and so she was held to be incompetent. The operation was ordered. (*Quaere*: does being in labour reduce a woman's capacity to make rational decisions any more than a needle phobia, with the result that the medical profession takes over her decision-making powers?)

Kelly v Kelly (1997): Mr and Mrs Kelly separated and they were in the process of divorce when it became known that Mrs Kelly was pregnant. Mr Kelly was the father but Mrs Kelly decided to seek an abortion. Mr Kelly objected and he sought an interdict to prevent her from going through with the termination. He claimed that he had title as the child's guardian and also in his own right.

The court held that a foetus has no "right" to remain in the mother's womb and so, if the abortion were carried out lawfully under the Abortion Act 1967, there would be no legally recognised loss that could be prevented by interdict.

Paton v UK (1981): Mr Paton, like Mr Kelly, failed in his attempt in the UK courts to prevent his wife from aborting their child. He claimed this was an infringement of his Art 8 right to family life and of the unborn child's Art 2 right to life.

The European Court of Human Rights dismissed his claim: the interference in his right to family life was justified by the need to protect the rights of the mother; the Art 2 right is implicitly limited in the early stages of pregnancy in order to protect the life and health of the woman.

Goodwin v United Kingdom (2002): Christine Goodwin had been born a male in 1937 but had undergone gender reassignment surgery as an adult. Since UK law at that time did not recognise sex change, this left her in an anomalous and embarrassing situation – she lived her life looking and acting as a female but (for example in employment contexts) was sometimes obliged to reveal her legal status as male. When she complained to the European Court of Human Rights, that court reversed its earlier decisions and held that the UK's refusal to recognise in legal terms the social reality of her changed gender amounted to an infringement of Art 8 of the European Convention on Human Rights (ECHR) (right to private life) and also of Art 12 (right to marry).

2 CREATING THE PARENT–CHILD RELATIONSHIP

The parent–child relationship comes into existence, in its fullest sense, when the child is born. The vast majority of children are born as a result of an act of sexual intercourse between their parents, but a growing number of children are conceived by other means, such as artificial insemination, in vitro fertilisation or embryo transfer. The legal parent–child relationship does not always reflect the genetic connection between the child and the producer of the sperm and egg from which he or she was created. This is so even when the child is born as a result of sexual intercourse. Court order can also create an artificial parent–child relationship.

CREATION THROUGH SEXUAL INTERCOURSE

When a child has been born as a result of sexual intercourse between a man and a woman the law deems the mother to be the woman who conceives with her eggs and gives birth to the child, and it presumes the father to be either (i) the man who is married to the mother at the moment of birth (or was married to her at any time between conception and birth) or (ii) the man who has acknowledged the child as his and who is registered in the Register of Births as the father of the child (Law Reform (Parent and Child) (Scotland) Act 1986, s 5). The presumption of paternity is rebuttable, by proof on the balance of probabilities either that the mother's husband is not, or that some other man is, the genetic father of the child. In cases of doubt this is today usually fairly easily established by means of a DNA test on both the child and the man alleged to be (or not to be) the father. But until the presumption is rebutted in a court of law the husband will be treated for all purposes as the father of the child, even when in fact he is not. If the mother is not married, and no man is registered as the father, the child is *not* legally fatherless: rather there is simply no man who is presumed to be the father. But paternity can be established in the same way as the presumption of paternity can be rebutted, that is to say by evidence on the balance of probabilities.

In order to determine paternity through DNA testing appropriate consents must, of course, be given. If the child is too young to consent then his or her legal representative may do so on the child's behalf – even if that legal representative holds that post only by operation of the presumption of paternity. If the adult refuses to give a sample for DNA analysis the court is empowered by s 70 of the Law Reform (Miscellaneous Provisions) (Scotland) Act 1990 to request the person to provide the sample, and a refusal to comply with the court's request will justify the court in drawing adverse inferences against the refusing party. The Scottish courts have, however, been resistant to drawing any conclusions of fact from such refusal.

CREATION THROUGH INFERTILITY TREATMENT

When a woman becomes pregnant through some form of infertility treatment, the law deems her to be the mother when she gives birth to the child (Human Fertilisation and Embryology Act 2008, s 33): this is so even when she has no genetic link to the child (for example when she becomes pregnant through implantation in her of an embryo created with another woman's egg). So the woman who gives birth to a child is always and for all purposes the mother of that child. Sometimes infertility treatment involves using sperm from a donor, and in that situation the law will deem the mother's partner (if she has one) to be the father of the child (if the partner is male), or a parent of the child (if the partner is female).

The application of this rule is slightly different depending upon whether or not the mother is married/civilly empartnered to her partner. If she is married/civilly empartnered to her partner, then the partner is deemed to be the father/parent of the child unless it can be shown that he or she did not consent to the infertility treatment that led to the mother becoming pregnant (2008 Act, ss 35 and 42). If she is not married/civilly empartnered to her partner, then the partner is deemed to be the father/parent of the child if the partner and the mother both gave written consent (not subsequently withdrawn) that the partner will be treated as the father/parent (2008 Act, ss 36 and 43). In the latter situation, however, there is an additional requirement, which is that the treatment must have been provided in the course of licensed treatment services provided by someone authorised to do so by the Human Fertilisation and Embryology Authority. The effect of this extra qualification is that "do-it-yourself" insemination of an unmarried/unempartnered woman (or any assisted reproduction procedure carried out beyond the borders of the UK) does not confer parenthood on her partner; the fact that this extra qualification does not apply to married/civilly empartnered couples means that "do-it-yourself" insemination of a married/civilly empartnered woman (or insemination abroad) does confer parenthood on her partner (unless it is shown that he or she did not consent). In either situation parenthood cannot be removed from the mother's partner by showing that he or she has no genetic link, or that another man does have a genetic link, to the child, for the rules only apply when the partner has no such link. The donor of the sperm (that is to say, the man who does have the genetic link) is, in law, not the father if the donation was to a licensed clinic and he consented to his donation being used for the creation of a child.

There are two situations in which a child born through infertility treatment will be deemed to be legally the child of only one parent. The first is when the donor of the sperm has had his paternity cut off by the application of the above rule but the woman has no partner who can be deemed father/parent; the second is when the sperm or the embryo created with the sperm was "used" after the death of the provider of the sperm. "Used" means used to bring about a pregnancy. This second situation is designed to deal with the long-term storage of sperm or embryos, for during the period of storage the provider of the sperm may die. If that happens the winding up of that dead man's estate would otherwise have to be postponed until all his sperm, or embryos created with his sperm, had been used up. But even although the child is legally fatherless for all practical purposes, it is possible to register the dead man as the father, so long as it can be shown that he consented to this happening. That registration has no practical legal consequence.

CREATION THROUGH COURT ORDER

A parent–child relationship can be created through court order in two situations: a so-called "parental order" after a surrogacy arrangement (governed by s 54 of the Human Fertilisation and Embryology Act 2008) and, more commonly, an adoption order (governed by the Adoption and Children (Scotland) Act 2007).

Surrogacy: parental orders

A surrogacy arrangement, whereby a woman agrees to carry a child until birth and then to hand it over to a "commissioning couple" is not in itself illegal (though organisations making the arrangements on a commercial basis are criminalised) but the arrangement itself is not legally enforceable. So if the surrogate mother refuses to hand over the child once born, or the commissioning couple refuse to take the child (because, for example, it is not as pretty as they had hoped), or they refuse to pay the "expenses" they had agreed after receiving the child, there is no legal redress on the part of anyone.

If, however, the arrangement is carried out as planned the commissioning couple will not both be the parents of the child, even although it is they who will be bringing up the child. The mechanism for transferring parenthood from the surrogate to the commissioning couple is by means of a parental order made under the 2008 Act. A parental order may be applied for by a married/civilly empartnered couple or by two persons living as partners in an enduring family relationship who are not within the prohibited degrees of relationship (parents, grandparents, siblings, uncles and aunts). The couple must apply for the order within six months of the birth of the child, one or other of them must be the genetic parent of the child, the surrogate mother must not have been paid a fee (though reasonable expenses are permitted) and she (and any other parent of the child) must freely consent to the making of the order. If the surrogate mother refuses to part with the child once it is born then there is nothing the commissioning couple can do about it, and if the child has been given up but the surrogate mother refuses to consent to the parental order, again there is nothing that can be done. She is the mother, since she is the one who gave birth to the child. The court has the power to authorise any fees beyond expenses that are paid, and it has readily done so (retrospectively), so long as they are reasonable – and relatively modest – notwithstanding the general prohibition on paying fees.

Adoption orders

To a large extent the parental order and its effects mirror the rules for adoption, though these are rather more complex and designed to deal with a very different type of case. Surrogacy followed by a parental order is the deliberate creation of a child in order to allow a couple to bring that child up; adoption deals with a child who already exists. The key to understanding adoption is to recognise that the adoption order does two things: it creates a parent–child relationship and, by definition, it simultaneously destroys the pre-existing parent–child relationship that came into existence on the child's birth. The latter effect is the main motivation for most adoptions today, which is thereafter an aspect of the child care and protection system which is activated when the existing parent–child relationship is operating in a manner that is detrimental to the interests of the child. This is discussed further in Chapter 5 below.

Adoption is also used as a means of family reconstitution, when a step-parent seeks to become the legal parent of the child of his or her spouse/civil partner. Here, too, the primary effect of the order is to destroy the existing parent–child relationship, though with step-parent adoption the spouse/civil partner of the adopter retains parenthood while it is the other parent (the non-resident parent) who has his parenthood removed. Any family reconstitution that does not intend to exclude the non-resident parent in this way is not adoption.

There are rules governing who may be adopted and who may adopt. In Scots law only a child may be adopted, and this is defined to mean for this purpose a person under the age of 18 years (though it is possible for the order to be made after the person's 18th birthday if the process began before that date). If the child is over 12 years old then his or her consent is necessary and without that consent the adoption cannot go ahead – the older child in Scotland has an absolute veto to his or her adoption. Even below the age of 12, the child's views must be taken into account in determining whether to grant the adoption order. The child must be at least 19 weeks old and have lived with the prospective adopters at all times during the preceding 13 weeks if the adopter is a relative or the child has been placed with the adopter by an adoption agency; otherwise the child must be at least 1 year old at the time of the making of the order. A married/civilly empartnered couple may adopt jointly, as may any unmarried/unempartnered couple in an "enduring family relationship". A single person may adopt a child, but a married person or civil partner may not adopt other than jointly with his or her spouse, unless the spouse cannot be found or is incapable through ill health of adopting, or the spouses/civil partners are permanently separated.

Given that the adoption order will destroy the existing parent–child relationship, it can be made only if either the existing parents consent to the adoption or their consent has been dispensed with by the court. The grounds for dispensing with the parents' agreement (Adoption and Children (Scotland) Act 2007, s 31) are as follows:

(a) that the parent is dead;
(b) that the parent cannot be found or is incapable of giving consent;
(c) that the parent is unable satisfactorily to fulfil parental responsibilities;
(d) that the parent has no parental responsibilities because they have been removed by the making of a permanence order;
(e) that, if (c) or (d) does not apply, the welfare of the child otherwise requires.

If one or more of these grounds exists the court must then decide whether it is in the interests of the child that parental agreement should be dispensed with.

Once the appropriate consents and agreements have been obtained the court will appoint various officers to examine the case, interview the child and prospective parents, and take account of the reports these officers produce in deciding whether to make an adoption order. The paramount consideration for the court in making an adoption order is the welfare of the child (2007 Act, s 14), though the adoption agency must also explore the extent to which an order less severe than an adoption order will achieve the purpose of securing the welfare of the child.

An adoption order, once made, is (subject only to the normal appeal process) final and irrevocable, except in limited circumstances such as when the order has been obtained by fraud or was made incompetently (for example over an adult).

Essential Facts

- A child's father is presumed to be the man who is either married to the mother or is registered as the father.
- When a child is born to a married or civilly empartnered woman after infertility treatment, the mother's partner is deemed to be the father/parent unless he or she did not consent to the treatment.
- When a child is born after licensed infertility treatment to an unmarried woman who is not in a civil partnership, the mother's unregistered partner is deemed to be the father/parent if they both consented to the partner being that parent.
- A "parental order" transfers parenthood from a surrogate mother to a commissioning couple, so long as one of the couple is genetically the parent of the child.
- An adoption order destroys the parenthood of the birth parents and creates parenthood in the adopters.
- A child of 12 or more must consent before an adoption order is made.

Essential Statutes

Law Reform (Parent and Child) (Scotland) Act 1986

Section 5 sets out two presumptions of paternity. Section 5(4) provides that the presumptions of paternity may be rebutted on the balance of probabilities.

Law Reform (Miscellaneous Provisions) (Scotland) Act 1990

Section 70 allows the court to request that any party in civil proceedings provide a sample, or consent to taking a sample from the child, for DNA analysis, and provides that if the party fails to do so the court may draw adverse inferences.

Human Fertilisation and Embryology Act 2008

Section 33 defines "mother" as the woman who is carrying or has carried the child. Sections 35 and 42 deem the mother's husband (or wife or civil partner) to be the father (or other parent) of the child if the mother became pregnant by the placing in her of the embryo, or of sperm and eggs, or her artificial insemination – but the husband, wife or civil partner will not be so deemed if he or she can show that he or she did not consent to the placing in the mother of the embryo, and so on. Sections 36 and 43 deem the mother's partner (who is not her husband, wife or civil partner) to be the father or (if female) other parent of the child so long as the infertility treatment was carried out by licensed providers and both the mother and her partner agreed to the partner becoming the child's father or other parent. Section 54 allows the court to make a parental order transferring parenthood from a surrogate mother to the commissioning couple, so long as various specified conditions are satisfied.

Adoption and Children (Scotland) Act 2007

Section 40 provides that on the making of an adoption order the child is to be treated in law as if born as the child of the adopters and as not being the child of any other person.

Essential Cases

Smith v Greenhill (1994): Anthony Smith raised an action against Elaine Greenhill, seeking declarator that her daughter was his child. Mrs Greenhill was married to another man and had other children. She refused to provide a sample for DNA analysis and Mr Smith asked the court to draw an adverse inference from that refusal.

The sheriff principal refused to draw any inference. The evidence showed that Mrs Greenhill had been having sex with both her husband and Mr Smith at the relevant time, but that the law presumed her husband to be the father of her child. Her refusal to undergo DNA analysis did not overturn that presumption.

Leeds Teaching Hospital NHS Trust v A & Ors (2003): after infertility treatment a white couple gave birth to a child who was clearly of mixed race. Investigation established that there had been a mix-up at the infertility clinic and that the sperm of a black man (who with his wife was also undergoing infertility treatment at the same clinic) had been mixed up with that of the white man. Who was the father of the child? The matter turned on the interpretation of s 28(2) of the Human Fertilisation and Embryology Act 1990 (now s 35(1) of the Human Fertilisation and Embryology Act 2008), which provides that the husband of a woman who becomes pregnant as a result of infertility treatment is the father, unless it can be shown that he did not consent to the treatment.

The court held that the white man had not consented to his wife being impregnated with the sperm of the black man therefore the mother's husband was not the father. Since the Act did not provide the answer, genetics did so and the black man was the father. The parties, good people all, had previously agreed that the child should remain with the white couple: the case might have been substantially more difficult had the black couple sought possession of what the court declared to be the black man's child or the white couple sought to make the black man liable for child support.

Evans v United Kingdom (2006): Ms Natallie Evans and Mr Howard Johnston were a couple attempting to have a child via infertility treatment. Embryos were created with the sperm of Mr Johnston and the eggs of Ms Evans (who could thereafter produce no more). Before they were implanted into Ms Evans the couple separated and Mr Johnston withdrew his consent to the embryos being used for the purpose of creating babies. Without consent the clinic could not release the embryos and they would have to be destroyed. Ms Evans sought to have this rule declared a breach of her right to found a family.

The court held that she did not have a right to found a family in circumstances which imposed family life on another person against his wishes. Any right she had to use the embryos was no stronger than Mr Johnston's right to refuse to allow them to be used. She could, in any case, still become a mother by using another woman's eggs and finding another man to fertilise them.

C v S (1996): Mr and Mrs C agreed with Ms S that Ms S would be artificially inseminated with Mr C's sperm, become pregnant, bear a child and give up the child to Mr and Mrs C on its birth, on the understanding that the couple would seek a parental order under the Human Fertilisation and Embryology Act 1990 and the mother would agree (as was required by that Act). The price was £8,000. The child was born, the money was paid and the birth was registered by Ms S naming Mr C as the father. Mr and Mrs C took the child home. Ms S then changed her mind and wanted her child back. Mr and Mrs C applied to adopt the child. The sheriff held that the payment of £8,000 contravened the Adoption (Scotland) Act 1978 and also the Human Fertilisation and Embryology Act 1990 and so he could make no order under either Act. But he made a residence order in favour of Mr and Mrs C and refused contact with Ms S.

On appeal the Court of Session held that the sheriff had been wrong to hold himself unable to make an adoption order: the £8,000 had been paid for the mother to consent to a parental order but not an adoption order and so there was no contravention of the Adoption (Scotland) Act. The adoption order was made in favour of Mr and Mrs C.

Re X and anor (Children) (Parental Order: Foreign Surrogacy) (2009): a Ukrainian woman agreed to act as a surrogate for an English couple, in return for a monthly payment and a lump sum of €25,000. Such payments were lawful in Ukraine, but unlawful in the UK unless authorised by the court.

The English High Court held that in deciding whether to authorise payments the court should ask itself three questions: (i) was the sum paid disproportionate to reasonable expenses?; (ii) were the commissioning couple acting in good faith and without "moral taint" in their dealings with the surrogate mother?; and (iii) were the commissioning couple party to any attempt to defraud the authorities? In the present case there had been no exploitation of the surrogate mother and though the surrogacy arrangement had been made in Ukraine rather than the UK (where payments were not permitted but where it was intended the child would be brought up) this did not amount to an attempt to defraud the authorities. The court retrospectively authorised the payment and made the parental order.

Re Z (A Child) (2013): a male couple agreed to provide some sperm to a female couple, though the parties never clarified with each other what the relationships would be. Children were born to the women and the men expected far greater involvement in the lives of these children than the women had either contemplated or were comfortable with. After some years of disagreement the men went to court seeking parental responsibility and contact. But the women were in a civil partnership and so were both the legal parents of the children: the men's paternity had been cut off by the Human Fertilisation and Embryology Act 2008. This meant (in England) that the men needed court leave to seek their orders.

The court granted the men leave on the ground that whatever the Act said the men were still the children's biological fathers.

Re B (Adoption Order: Jurisdiction to set aside) (1995): a young man who had been adopted as a child by a Jewish couple sought to have the adoption order revoked after the death of his adoptive parents, on the basis that they had been defrauded into adopting him by having been told that he was Jewish when in fact he was an Arab. The court dismissed this claim and held that only in the most exceptional circumstances could a court revoke an adoption order, such as deliberate and bad faith fraud which did not exist in this case.

Webster v Norfolk County Council (2009): A child suffered unexplained broken bones and when all known medical explanations were ruled out the local authority concluded that the parents were to blame. The child was removed and placed for adoption, and later adopted. The parents then had another child who suffered similarly, but at this point it was discovered that the child was suffering from scurvy, which would explain the earlier child's broken bones. The parents asked for the return of their earlier child.

The court held that notwithstanding the new evidence which might indicate that the child had been removed from its parents for no good reason, it would be against the interests of that child for the adoption order now to be rescinded. It is only in very exceptional circumstances that an adoption order, once made, can ever be put aside.

Scott v United Kingdom (2000): an alcoholic woman gave birth to a baby girl who was suffering from foetal alcohol syndrome. After treatment, the baby was allowed to be taken home by the mother. The mother's alcohol abuse continued and she was unable to care for the child properly so the father (who was not married to the mother) took the child to the social services department of the local authority and left her there. The local authority placed the child with foster carers and sought to help the mother address her alcohol problems. After two-and-a-half years it was obvious that no progress was being made and the local authority then sought to free the child for adoption. The mother refused to agree but the court dispensed with her consent to adoption. She then took the British Government to the European Court of Human Rights, on the basis that her right to family life under Art 8 had been infringed by the dispensing with her agreement.

The European Court held that the decision-making process in this case had not denied the mother opportunities to participate, that there was no chance of her resuming care of her child while her alcoholism persisted, that there was no foreseeable chance of her being cured of alcoholism and that therefore although the decision of the domestic courts meant that her family life with her child would be terminated, this was a proportionate response to the problem. So there was no breach of Art 8.

3 BRINGING UP CHILDREN

Children have a right to be brought up by their parents, as defined by their own legal system (UN Convention on the Rights of the Child, Art 7), and both parents and children have a right to respect for their family life (European Convention on Human Rights, Art 8). By and large, parents are left free to determine how best to bring up their own children, but there are numerous duties that Scots law requires parents to fulfil, because the essence of the parent–child relationship is one of parental responsibility to bring up children properly: it ought not to be seen (though it often is) as one that confers rights on parents to bring up children the way they think fit. Parents are, however, for the most part, left to do just that. The law lays down a set of minimum standards, and failure to meet these standards may justify the state stepping in for the benefit of the child. These standards are contained in various statutes, such as the Children (Scotland) Act 1995, which sets out in fairly general terms the parental responsibilities and parental rights that the law imposes on parents; the Family Law (Scotland) Act 1985, which governs the obligation of parents to aliment (i.e. to provide financially for the child); and the various Education (Scotland) Acts which govern the obligations on parents to educate their children.

WHO IS OBLIGED TO FULFIL UPBRINGING DUTIES?

Because the various obligations imposed on parents are contained in different statutes, the person subject to these obligations is defined in each, and is defined differently.

Parental responsibilities and parental rights (Children (Scotland) Act 1995)

The responsibility and right to make decisions as to how a child is to be brought up is imposed not on all "parents", however defined, but only on those specified by s 3 of the Children (Scotland) Act 1995, that is to say (i) mothers, (ii) fathers who are registered as such in the Register of Births and (iii) other parents recognised under the Human Fertilisation and Embryology Act 2008 and registered as such. They may also be imposed on other persons (including unregistered fathers) if a parent nominates that person to be the child's guardian after the death of the parent under s 7 of the 1995 Act, or if a court makes an order under s 11 imposing parental responsibilities and parental rights on such a person, or if the mother agrees under s 4 or s 4A to share them with the father or the other female parent. The court must be motivated by the welfare of the child when deciding whether to make an order relating to the child's upbringing, but a parent or guardian making a will or an agreement does not need to be motivated by that factor.

Aliment and child support (Family Law (Scotland) Act 1985; Child Support Act 1991)

All parents legally defined as such, whether married to each other or not, or registered in the Register of Births or not, or living with the child or not, are obliged to maintain the child in a financial sense, by providing the child with aliment to the extent required by the Family Law (Scotland) Act 1985. The obligation of aliment is extended beyond parents and is imposed also on any person who has accepted the child as a member of his or her family even though he or she is not actually the parent of the child. So the step-parent or co-parent who has accepted the child as a member of his or her family is obliged to the same extent as the actual parent to aliment the child. The non-resident parent may also be liable for child support under the Child Support Act 1991, which provides a state-enforced mechanism to force parents to meet upbringing costs: child support is a financial obligation on parents only and is not imposed on all those who are obliged to aliment the child.

Education (Education (Scotland) Act 1981)

Again all parents are obliged to ensure that their children receive an efficient education, and again the obligation is extended beyond parents to include any person who has an obligation to maintain the child. So those obliged under this Act are the same as the people obliged to aliment the child under the Family Law (Scotland) Act 1985.

Other

There are some other obligations that are imposed on persons who happen to have children in their actual care even although they do not have a parent–child relationship (such as, typically, step-parents). Any person who has care or control of a child is obliged to protect the welfare of that child (Children (Scotland) Act 1995, s 5) and in particular may provide consent to the child's medical treatment. Similarly, any person who has or has recently had significant involvement in the upbringing of the child may be deemed to be a "relevant person" and so obliged to attend the children's hearing with the child under the terms of the Children's Hearings (Scotland) Act 2011 (discussed in Chapter 5 below).

PARENTAL RESPONSIBILITIES AND PARENTAL RIGHTS

The most important, in practical terms, of all the upbringing powers are the parental responsibilities and parental rights contained in the Children (Scotland) Act 1995. Section 1 of that Act sets out the parental responsibilities that parents must fulfil in their bringing up of children. These are as follows:

(1) the responsibility to safeguard and promote the child's health, development and welfare;
(2) the responsibility to provide the child with direction and guidance;
(3) the responsibility to maintain personal relations and direct contact with the child if the parent and child are not living together;
(4) the responsibility to act as the child's legal representative.

Section 2 of the 1995 Act sets out the parental rights that parents have in order to allow them to fulfil the responsibilities listed in s 1. These are as follows:

(1) the right to determine where the child is to reside;
(2) the right to control, direct and guide the child;
(3) the right to maintain personal relations and direct contact with the child if not living with the child;
(4) the right to act as the child's legal representative.

No responsibility or right can now be traced to the common law, and parents wishing to take any action in respect of the upbringing of the child must do so by reference to one or more of the above responsibilities or rights. Though it is usually the case that two persons will be sharing parental responsibilities and parental rights, either one may normally act without the consent of the other. Only one act always requires the consent of both parents, and that is the removal of the child from the United Kingdom.

Responsibility 1 is the broadest of all the responsibilities and rights and will govern most decisions that a parent must make. It rests with all parents who have parental responsibilities and not just those with Right 1. While it might be expected that a decision to safeguard the child's health, development and welfare will be in its best interests, there is much scope for disagreement. If parents agree on a particular matter then their decision will govern unless it is clearly harmful to the child. If the parents disagree, it is for the court to determine where the child's interests lie, through the procedures described in the next chapter.

Responsibility 2 needs to be read in the light of Right 2, and so the direction and guidance that the parent offers must be seen in light of the obligation to direct and guide. Responsibility 3 and Right 3 come into existence when the parent and the child are not living together. This might be because the parents have never lived together, or because they previously lived together but have since separated. In either case, it is the parental responsibility, and the child's right, that family life be maintained between the non-resident parent and the child, at least to the extent of direct contact between the two (and it is the responsibility of the residence parent to permit and encourage this contact to take place). Responsibility 4 and Right 4 together give the parent power to act in legal transactions on behalf of the child, though this power exists only while the child does not have legal capacity to act on his or her own behalf. The child may acquire such capacity before the age of 16 (as was seen in Chapter 1 above), in which case the parent loses the power to act as legal representative in the matter. When the parent does act as legal representative he or she must make decisions on the basis of the welfare of the child but, subject to that, has the power to do whatever the child, if of full age, could have done himself or herself.

ALIMENT

The obligation to aliment is the obligation to provide financially for the child. This was a common law obligation and is now contained in the first seven sections of the Family Law (Scotland) Act 1985. The obligation is to provide such support as is reasonable in the circumstances for the child's upkeep and it lasts until the child is 18 years old, or 25 years old if the child over 18 is undergoing full-time education (1985 Act, s 1(5)). The obligation is normally fulfilled by the parent providing housing, food and clothing for the child, and in legal terms it goes little beyond that. Most parents, of course, expend far more than the minimum demanded by the law. A claim for aliment in a court is usually made when the family has broken up and the now absent parent is not paying what the residence parent perceives as a fair share. But it is important to note that the obligation is not to provide a fair share of the full and actual upbringing costs but merely to provide the minimum the law requires.

An action for aliment is not competent in situations in which a claim for child support can be made, through the Child Support Agency and governed by the oft-amended Child Support Act 1991. This is designed to ensure a fair sharing of the real costs, though the technical details are too complex to go into here. In practice, however, since child support ends at 16, actions for aliment are today limited to claims by persons over that age and are commonly raised by students seeking parental contributions to their living expenses while at college or university.

EDUCATION

Children have a right to education (Standards in Scotland's Schools etc Act 2000) and parents have a duty to provide efficient education suitable to the child's age, ability and aptitude (Education (Scotland) Act 1980, s 30). Mostly this duty is fulfilled by sending a child to school, but the obligation is to provide education rather than to send the child to school and so if a parent can provide efficient education by other means, this is acceptable. It is an offence for the parent to fail to fulfil this duty without reasonable excuse. More recent legislation has emphasised the importance of parental choice of schools, but it has been remarkably silent on the issue of children's choice. Article 2 of Protocol 1 of the European Convention on Human Rights (ECHR) provides that no person shall be denied the right to education and that the state shall respect the right of parents to ensure such education and teaching in conformity with their own religious and philosophical convictions. So here again the issue of education is constructed around parents. Parents cannot, however, use their religious beliefs in the benefits of beating children to insist that the state allows corporal punishment of children in schools.

Essential Facts

- Parents are, by and large, left to bring up their own children as they think fit.
- Parental responsibilities and parental rights (PR & PR) attach to all mothers and to fathers and other female parents who are registered as the father or other female parent.
- All parents are obliged to bear the financial cost of bringing up their children, whether or not, in fact, they are involved in that upbringing.

- Either parent may exercise his or her PR & PR independently of the other, except that the consent of both is always needed to remove the child from the United Kingdom.
- Where parents agree, their own judgment as to where the child's interests lie will normally govern; where parents disagree, it is for the court to determine the child's welfare.
- Children have a legal right to be properly educated and it is a criminal offence for parents to fail to ensure that they receive it.

Essential Statutes

Children (Scotland) Act 1995

Section 1 sets out the parental responsibilities that parents are legally obliged to fulfil. Section 2 sets out the parental rights that parents enjoy in order to allow them to fulfil their parental responsibilities. Section 3 sets out who are the holders of parental responsibilities and parental rights. Sections 4 and 4A allow mothers to agree to share parental responsibilities and parental rights with the other parent of the child, where that other parent does not have parental responsibilities and parental rights under s 3.

Family Law (Scotland) Act 1985

Sections 1–7 set down the rule for aliment that a child may claim from a parent (where the Child Support Act 1991 does not apply).

Child Support Act 1991

This statute sets out, in very great detail, the circumstances in which a parent's obligation to support a child financially can be enforced by the state when the parent does not live with the child.

Education (Scotland) Act 1980

Section 30 provides that it is the duty of the parent of every child of school age to provide an education for him or her suitable to his or her age, ability and aptitude, either by causing the child to attend a public school regularly or by other means. Section 35 provides that the parent commits an offence if a child fails to attend school regularly without reasonable excuse.

Essential Cases

Gillick v West Norfolk & Wisbech Area Health Authority (1986): Mrs Gillick was the mother of ten children and wanted to decide everything about their upbringing, including their access to sexual health care, until they were 16. She sought a guarantee from the health authority that it would not provide any of her children with such health care without her knowledge and consent. The Health Authority refused to give this guarantee.

The House of Lords held that children were entitled to health care without their parent's agreement if they understood the nature of the treatment and (in English law) if it was in their interests to receive it. Parents have rights, they said, only in order to allow them to fulfil their responsibilities towards their children.

R v Secretary of State for Education, ex parte Williamson (2005): corporal punishment in British schools had been banned as a result of decisions of the European Court of Human Rights holding such punishment to be an infringement of, first, parents' philosophical convictions (as protected by Art 2 of Protocol 1 of the ECHR) not to have their children beaten and, secondly, of children's rights not to be subjected to inhuman or degrading treatment (as guaranteed by Art 3 of the ECHR). Teachers and parents at four Christian schools argued that this total ban on corporal punishment was incompatible with the ECHR since it was an infringement of *their* right to freedom of religion and freedom to manifest their religious beliefs by hitting children as punishment for their misdeeds.

The House of Lords held that, since non-violent means of discipline are available to teachers, a total ban on physical punishment was a proportionate balance between religious convictions and the need to protect children from undue violence.

Re J (2000): a child was born to a mixed marriage: his father was Muslim and his mother was non-Muslim. The parents separated and the child remained with the mother. The father then sought to ensure that the child was circumcised. The mother opposed this and the father raised an action to enforce his wishes.

The court held that in any situation in which the parents could not agree in respect of an issue of the upbringing of the child, the court had to determine the issue on the basis of what was in the child's best interests. In this case it was not in the child's best interests to be circumcised and so the father's action failed. Had the parents agreed, it would have been lawful to perform the circumcision that was not in the child's best interests.

Re C (A Child) (Immunisation: Parental Rights) (2003): a mother and estranged father disagreed as to whether their child should receive the MMR triple vaccine. The mother wanted to refuse consent and argued that it was for her as the child's primary carer to decide the issue by weighing up in her own mind the risks and benefits of this procedure.

The Court of Appeal held that in cases of parental disagreement the matter did not fall to the primary carer but was rather to be resolved by the court's assessment of what was in the child's interests. The fears of autism arising from the triple vaccine were dismissed by the court as "junk science" and they held that it was clearly in the child's interests to be given the vaccine: the real risks of measles, mumps or rubella were very significantly greater than a hypothetical risk of an injury that research suggested was negligible, if it existed at all.

Re A (Conjoined Twins: Medical Treatment) (2001): conjoined twins were born to a couple who held devout religious beliefs in the sanctity of life. The medical prognosis was that unless an attempt were made to separate the twins, neither would survive very long. The problem was that any attempt to save the better-developed child would most certainly kill the less-developed child. The parents were irreconcilably opposed to any procedure that would lead to the certain death of either twin. The Health Authority sought court authorisation to proceed with the separation, in the full knowledge that it would kill one twin.

The Court of Appeal held that the operation should go ahead. The best interests of the better-developed child required this and it was her only hope of life. The less-developed child would either die during the operation or die in any case, taking her sister with her, and so had no best interests to serve.

Crossan v South Lanarkshire Council (2006): the father of a 13-year-old boy who suffered from Down's Syndrome sought judicial review of a decision by the council not to fund after-school care for the child, notwithstanding that the child had been assessed under the Children (Scotland) Act 1995 as being in need of such care. The court held that the council had a discretion, but not a duty, to meet the needs of the child as identified in a needs assessment. So the action failed. In any case, the action was not so much about the child's needs as about who should pay for them – the parents or the local authority.

4 COURT ORDERS REGULATING THE UPBRINGING OF CHILDREN

The Court of Session and the sheriff court have the power to make orders in relation to parental responsibilities, parental rights, guardianship or the administration of a child's property (Children (Scotland) Act 1995, s 11). This will typically be when parents separate and they cannot agree on some matter such as, for example, with whom the child is to live, or how often the absent parent is to see the child, or whether the child should take a new name (such as the name of the residence parent's new partner), or whether the child should be allowed to accompany one parent who wishes to emigrate in pursuit of a new life; but an order might also be sought in a variety of circumstances in which the parents are not themselves separating. For example, the parents may be in disagreement as to how the child is to be educated, or what medical treatment he or she is to receive, or how property that the child has acquired should be administered. Though it is normally a dispute between parents that creates a court action, this may not always be the case and the court may be asked to resolve a dispute between a parent and grandparents, or between the parents and the child's medical advisers or even between the parents and the child him or herself.

THE OVERARCHING PRINCIPLES

However a dispute arises in relation to parental responsibilities, parental rights, guardianship or the administration of a child's property, the court is bound to decide that dispute by taking account of the three principles, sometimes referred to as "the overarching principles", contained in s 11(7) of the 1995 Act. These are as follows:

(1) The court must regard the welfare of the child as its paramount consideration. Other considerations may be relevant but the most important of all and the factor that will normally determine the case is the court's assessment of which decision will best further the child's welfare. Of course the welfare test on its own is meaningless without the court also bearing in mind a range of factors that affect (or at least are perceived to affect) the child's welfare and the court has no option but to make

its own assessment of the value of a number of factors – such as the importance of maintaining a link with the child's past, the relevance of domestic violence within the household, the value of continuity of relationships and now, of course, the necessity to ensure that the family life protected by Art 8 of the European Convention is properly respected. The only matter that the court is explicitly required to have regard to in determining the child's welfare is the need to protect the child from any domestic abuse or risk of domestic abuse, either direct or indirect (i.e. towards the child or another family member): 1995 Act, s 11(7A)–(7E), as inserted by s 24 of the Family Law (Scotland) Act 2006.

(2)   The court is obliged to make no order unless it considers that it would be better for the child that the order be made than that none should be made at all. This is the so-called "no-order principle" under which the court must be positively persuaded that making an order will in fact further the child's best interests. This is an important brake on unnecessary orders and is a recognition that it may often be the case that the sorts of disputes that are mentioned above cannot be satisfactorily resolved by court decree. Parliament has given guidance with this principle that, wherever possible, matters should be regulated by the parties without the intervention of the courts. This principle reflects the "proportionality" principle in European Human Rights law, whereby state interference in private or family life is legitimate only insofar as it is proportionate to the aim sought to be achieved.

(3)   Taking account of the child's age and maturity, the court shall so far as practicable give the child the opportunity to indicate whether he or she wishes to express any views on the matter in dispute; if the child indicates that he or she does wish to express views, give him or her the opportunity to do so; and have regard to these views. This obligation can be traced to Art 12 of the UN Convention on the Rights of the Child. It is not an obligation to give effect to the child's views and no child has the right to decide the matter before the court. Rather, it is considered proper that the court take account of such views as the child is willing to express, but always bearing in mind the court's primary obligation to decide the case with the child's welfare being the paramount consideration. The older and more (mentally) mature the child is, the less likely it is that the court will go against his or her wishes, but that is not because the child

has a right to decide but because the older the child is, the more likely it will not be in his or her welfare to be made to do something he or she does not wish to do. A child who is 12 years of age or over shall be presumed to be of sufficient maturity to form a view (1995 Act, s 11(10)), but this does not mean that children under 12 are presumed to be of insufficient maturity. Rather, each child has to be considered individually and taking account of the complexity of the issue at hand.

THE AVAILABLE ORDERS

The court has a variety of orders at its disposal, and they are listed in s 11(2) of the 1995 Act:

(1) An order depriving a person of some or all of his or her parental responsibilities and parental rights. Remembering the "no-order principle", this provision must be utilised if a person is to lose any aspect of his or her power to be involved in the bringing up of the child. Merely to stop living with the child, even when that living arrangement is sanctioned by the court, does not in itself deprive the non-resident parent of any parental responsibility or parental right and so he (for typically the absent parent is the father rather than the mother) is still fully entitled to be involved in the decision-making processes relating to the child's education, medical treatment and any other aspect of upbringing. Only an order under this provision actively depriving a parent of parental responsibilities will give the residence parent the right to make decisions on her own. And, bearing in mind the "welfare principle", it will have to be shown why an order depriving a non-resident (or any other) parent of some aspect of parental responsibility is in the child's best interests – the court will not assume that it is best for a child that the residence parent have exclusive decision-making power (but it is of course open to have this proved). In this way the law tries to encourage both parents even after separation to remain fully involved in their children's lives – though many residence parents resent this continued involvement because it is necessarily an involvement in their own lives too.

(2) An order imposing parental responsibilities or giving parental rights. This will be appropriate when the person who is in fact caring for the child and is actively involved in the child's

upbringing does not in law have any parental responsibilities or parental rights. This might be, for example, a grandparent with whom the child lives because of the parents' incapacity, absence or death. Or it might be the residence parent's new partner (a step-parent or co-parent) who drives the child to school every day and helps with the child's homework every evening, and who seeks to persuade the court that it is in the child's best interests that he be involved in schooling decisions. It should be noted that there is no limit on the number of persons who may hold at any one time parental responsibilities and parental rights and so an order granting a co-parent such responsibilities and rights does not take them away from any other person (such as the absent parent). Removal of parental responsibilities would, as we have seen, require to be sought under para (1) above.

(3) An order regulating the arrangements as to with whom, or with whom during what periods, the child is to live. This is known as a residence order and is most frequently sought on parental separation where both parents want the child to live with him or her. An order under this paragraph does no more (bearing in mind the "no-order principle") than it says: in other words, it merely regulates where the child is to live and it does not give exclusive decision-making rights, or even precedence, to the parent who is granted residence of the child (as the pre-1995 law, which used the terminology of "custody", was assumed to do). The court can make an order in a variety of different ways here, such as requiring the child to live with one parent all the time and never with the other, or with one parent during the week and the other during the weekend, or with one parent during school term-time and the other during school vacations. The court may require the child to live with someone other than parents, such as, for example, a grandparent or even an elder sibling: if it does so, then full parental responsibilities and parental rights are carried with the residence order (1995 Act, s 11(12)).

(4) An order regulating the arrangements for maintaining personal relations and direct contact between the child and a person with whom the child is not living. This is known as a contact order and will be used typically to regulate the arrangements for the non-resident parent after parental separation to see the child on a regular basis. Again, this order does no more than it says: it regulates arrangements. There is no limitation on who can benefit from a contact order and so while usually it will be

designed to regulate contact between the child and an absent father, it can also regulate contact between the child and a grandparent, sibling (even if under 16), other relative or a friend or neighbour. As with a residence order, the court is given maximum flexibility to make any order that it deems to be in the interests of the child. It should be noted, however, that court orders have a tendency to freeze arrangements and an arrangement that was suitable when the parents separate may not be suitable for the child even a year or two later when he or she is older, more independent and with new friends, interests and activities. Courts are aware of this and, also because of the "no-order principle" discussed above, will need to be persuaded that making the order really is best for the child.

(5) An order regulating any specific question that has arisen. This is known as a "specific issue order" and is primarily designed to deal with one-off issues rather than the continuing issue of residence or contact. So, if there is a dispute as to, for example, the child's medical treatment, education, religious upbringing or name, the court may be asked to resolve the dispute (by determining what would be best for the child) under this paragraph.

(6) An interdict. This would be appropriate to prevent someone doing something, even when it is otherwise within his or her rights to do so, whenever the applicant can show to the satisfaction of the court that the defender's intention would be harmful to the child's interests. So, a parent may be interdicted from removing the child from the jurisdiction if this is considered dangerous, or from subjecting the child to untried and experimental medical treatment, or from being brought up within the confines of a religion whose practices are socially isolating or otherwise considered damaging.

(7) An order appointing a judicial factor. A judicial factor is a court officer who controls property on behalf of another and an order under this paragraph would be useful, therefore, whenever the child comes to own a significant amount of money which the parents for some reason (for example, due to financial inexperience) ought not to be left to look after.

(8) An order appointing or removing a person as guardian. A person may be appointed as guardian (or parent-substitute) of the child by a parent or guardian in his or her will to act after the death of the parent or guardian. A testamentary appointment is not limited by the "best interests test", but the court can be asked

to remove such a guardian under this paragraph if it is not in the child's interests for guardianship under that person to continue. The court can also make an appointment of its own under this paragraph, even before the parent or guardian dies.

TITLE TO SEEK AN ORDER

Any of these orders may be sought by any person who either has parental responsibilities and parental rights or claims an interest in the child and his or her welfare. Indeed the court may make a s 11 order of its own volition and does not need to wait until it is asked (though there does need to be some issue before the civil court in any case during which the court comes to believe that an order would further the child's welfare). The child too can him or herself make an application for a s 11 order: children have capacity to sue in the civil courts whenever they have a general understanding of what it means to do so (Age of Legal Capacity (Scotland) Act 1991, s 2(4A)). So a child may seek an order removing a parent from decision-making powers, or an order requiring or allowing him or her to live with one of the parents or even someone else entirely.

There are two categories of person who cannot seek a s 11 order. First, and more straightforwardly, are local authorities. Their powers to become involved in the upbringing of children are extensive but highly constrained and are contained in very detailed provisions in the public law sections found in Part 2 of the Children (Scotland) Act 1995, in the Adoption and Children (Scotland) Act 2007 and in the Children's Hearings (Scotland) Act 2011. Local authorities cannot avoid these detailed provisions (discussed in Chapter 5 below) by seeking an order under the much more straightforward s 11 (which is found in the private law Part 1 of the 1995 Act). Secondly, any person who used to have parental responsibilities and parental rights but from whom such responsibilities and rights were removed by the adoption or permanence process under the Adoption and Children (Scotland) Act 2007 or the making of a parental order under the Human Fertilisation and Embryology Act 2008 cannot seek to have them restored by the straightforward provisions in s 11, except that in the case of an adoption order the court may grant leave to seek the order. These limitations do not apply to individuals whose responsibilities and rights were earlier removed by an order under s 11 itself. So, for example, a non-resident parent who is deprived of parental responsibilities and parental rights by an order under s 11(2)(a) has title to seek their restoration and he or she might be successful if, say, circumstances have changed since that order was made.

Essential Facts

- All disputes between individuals in relation to the upbringing of children are to be resolved with the child's welfare being the paramount consideration.
- The child must always be given an opportunity to express views on the dispute and the court must not make any order unless it considers that it would be better for the child to do so than not to do so.
- Both parents' PRs & PRs continue after parental separation.
- A child as much as a parent has title to seek a s 11 order to regulate any aspect of his or her upbringing.
- A parent whose PR & PR have been removed by an adoption order cannot seek their restoration by means of a s 11 order except that a contact order may be sought with leave of the court.

Essential Statutes

Children (Scotland) Act 1995

Section 11(1) allows the court to regulate how a parent brings up a child by making an order relating to parental responsibilities, parental rights, guardianship or the administration of the child's property. Section 11(2) lists the specific orders that a court may make. Section 11(3) allows the court to make a s 11 order even when not asked to do so, or when asked to do so by someone who either has parental responsibilities or parental rights in relation to the child, or who claims an interest. Section 11(3) and (4) prevents the order from being sought by anyone whose parental responsibilities and parental rights have been removed by an adoption order or a parental order after surrogacy, except that after an adoption order an ex-parent may seek leave of the court to apply for a contact order. Section 11(5) prevents a s 11 order being sought by a local authority. Section 11(7) sets out the three "overarching principles" that a court must apply in deciding whether to make a s 11 order. Section 11(7A) and (7B) includes within the paramountcy of welfare (one of the overarching principles) the requirement to take account of the need to protect the child from domestic abuse.

Essential Cases

Brixey v Lynas (1996): Emma Brixey was a teenage single mother when she met the schoolboy Michael Lynas who was attending a boarding school close to where she lived and worked. They started having sex, Emma became pregnant and a little girl was born when Emma was 20 and Michael was 18. After living for a short period of time together with Michael's parents, the relationship broke down and Emma returned north. Michael then raised an action for custody (now called "residence") of the little girl, and the sheriff granted him custody on the basis that Mrs Lynas (Michael's mother and the child's grandmother) would be better able to look after the girl than the flighty, immature Emma. The Inner House overruled this on the ground that the sheriff had failed to take account of the need of a young child for its mother. Michael appealed to the House of Lords on the basis that the Inner House had placed too much emphasis on a "maternal preference".

The House of Lords held that while there is no rule of law or principle or presumption that very young children should remain with their mothers, it was nevertheless a fact of nature which had to be taken into account that a very young child's need for his or her mother is usually greater than his or her need for the father. The child stayed with her mother.

Osborne v Matthan (No 2) (1998): Althea Matthan was a native of Jamaica. She came to the United Kingdom where she supported herself and her young daughter, Fiona, through prostitution and drug-dealing. When Fiona was 2, Althea was imprisoned in England and she asked her neighbour and (then) friend Mrs Helen Osborne to look after Fiona on her behalf. Three years later, when Althea was about to be released from jail, it became apparent that on her release she would be deported back to Jamaica. At this stage Mrs Osborne moved to Perth and sought a residence order to retain Fiona and to prevent her being returned to her mother, and so returned to Jamaica. The sheriff awarded residence to Mrs Osborne and Althea appealed against that decision.

The Inner House held that the decision had to stand. Though mothers have primary rights in disputes with strangers the fundamental issue is always what is in the best interests of the child and here it was clear that Mrs Osborne could give Fiona a much better upbringing than the indigent and homeless Ms Matthan who was on the brink of being deported to a poverty-stricken country.

Porchetta v Porchetta (1986): Mr and Mrs Porchetta divorced when their child was very young. Mrs Porchetta was awarded what was then called custody of the child and Mr Porchetta sought what was then called access to his child, now called "contact". Mrs Porchetta was hostile to her ex-husband and his presence was causing her, and consequently the child, distress: she refused to allow him to see the child. Mr Porchetta went to court for an access order on the basis that he was entitled to access with his own child.

The court held that so-called parental "rights" are not rights in the sense of being automatically enforceable, and that he had to prove that it would be in the welfare of the child to grant the order sought.

White v White (2001): Mr and Mrs White separated, their two children remaining with Mrs White. Mr White had generous contact with his daughters, until he entered into a relationship with a new woman. The new woman fell out with Mrs White who thereafter refused to allow Mr White contact with the girls. He raised an action seeking a contact order. At first instance, the sheriff held that since the Children (Scotland) Act 1995 was based on the assumption that contact with both parents should continue, that should be his starting point. In other words, the onus was on Mrs White to show why contact should be stopped. On appeal the sheriff principal disagreed and held that the "no-order principle" or "minimum intervention principle" in the 1995 Act placed the onus on the person seeking the order (Mr White) to show that it would be beneficial to make the order. Mr White appealed to the Court of Session.

That court held that there was no onus one way or the other. The court had to weigh up whether it was or was not in the interests of the child to have the order made. The so-called "minimum intervention principle" was simply an indication that Parliament believed that it was better that children did not have unnecessary orders over them.

A v B (Alternative Families) (2012): a gay man agreed with his friends, a lesbian couple, to provide sperm so that they could have a child. It was agreed that he would be recognised as the father, but would play a secondary role in the upbringing of the child. When they all fell out, the man sought a contact order and the women sought a joint residence order. The judge at first instance granted both orders, indicating that the nuclear family was not to be threatened by overnight contact. The father appealed.

The Court of Appeal allowed the appeal and held that the only principle to govern such cases was the welfare of the child. Cases involving female couples and male donors were all different and not to be treated as similar; nor were they similar to the case of a divorced father seeking contact with his child who lives with the mother and her new partner. Each case is fact specific. The Court also indicated that it was unhelpful to characterise (as the judge had done) known donors as "secondary parents" and the main carers of the child as "primary parents".

Sanderson v McManus (1997): Stuart Sanderson raised an action against Jane McManus for paternity and access in relation to a little boy, Bradley. Jane did not dispute Stuart's paternity claim but she resisted allowing him any access to their son. Interim access was permitted before the case went to proof but during that time the boy, then aged 4, alleged that his father had hit him and at the proof further access was denied. The case went to the House of Lords.

The court held that while the boy's evidence could not be taken as proof of what he said (because of his age), the boy's behaviour was a matter to be taken into account. The father's claim for access had to be based on more than the fact that he was the father: the question was always whether contact was likely to benefit the child and the sheriff's decision that there was no benefit could not be criticised by an appeal court. So the father lost access.

M v M (2012): Mr and Mrs M had had two children when they separated. Mrs M entered a relationship with a new man, who lived in Berkshire, England, and she sought the court's permission to remove the children to that location (Mr M refusing consent). Though given such permission at first instance, this was overturned on appeal.

The Inner House held that the English approach to requests for permission to relocate did not represent the law of Scotland. In England, residence parents tend to be granted permission to relocate the child to another country if the plans are not unreasonable. The Inner House considered that this amounted to a presumption in favour of relocation. In Scotland, the decision must be made without any presumption, for each case is different and the welfare of the child is the only criterion that is to be applied: previous cases in this area set no precedent. In the instant case, the mother had not shown that, on balance, it would be better for the child to be relocated to Berkshire than to remain in a familiar location and so she was refused permission to take the child to live in Berkshire.

5 STATE INTERVENTION IN THE UPBRINGING OF CHILDREN

As we have seen, although Scots law by and large allows parents and others with parental responsibilities and parental rights to determine how their children are to be brought up, there are various obligations imposed on parents and various expectations as to how they will fulfil their duties. Similarly, although Scots law is obliged by Art 8 of the European Convention on Human Rights to respect the right to family life inhering in both parent and child, the state is also obliged to ensure that children are not subjected to abuse, neglect, torture and inhuman or degrading treatment. Since the horrible truth is that far more children suffer in this way at the hands of their own parents than at the hands of strangers, it follows that, in order to fulfil its duty towards children, the state is sometimes obliged to act against the parents and to require that children are subjected to care and protection measures against the wishes of their own parents. The power of the state to do so is contained in a number of provisions, the most important of which is the Children's Hearings (Scotland) Act 2011. But other Acts to take note of are the Children and Young Persons (Scotland) Act 1937, which makes it an offence to neglect a child to such an extent that he or she is likely to suffer significant harm; the Matrimonial Homes (Family Protection) (Scotland) Act 1981, which allows for the granting of matrimonial and other interdicts against the owner or occupier of a property in which the child lives when this is necessary for the safety of the child; the Protection from Abuse (Scotland) Act 2001, which allows the court to attach powers of arrest to interdicts (that is to say, allows the police to become involved in the enforcement of the civil remedy of interdict); the Protection of Children (Scotland) Act 2003, which obliges organisations who deal with children to carry out police checks on those employed by the organisations; the Antisocial Behaviour etc (Scotland) Act 2004, which permits the courts to make "parenting orders" over parents whose upbringing skills are wanting; and the Adoption and Children (Scotland) Act 2007, which allows the court to remove a child permanently from the parents, by means of either a permanence order (discussed below) or an adoption order (discussed below and in Chapter 2 above). The most important procedural mechanism for protecting children is the children's hearing system, for that quasi-judicial tribunal is the busiest tribunal in

Scotland and it makes far more public law orders over children than the courts do.

THE CHILDREN'S HEARING SYSTEM

The children's hearing system is uniquely Scottish. It was established by the Social Work (Scotland) Act 1968 and underwent significant modification by the Children (Scotland) Act 1995 and the Children's Hearings (Scotland) Act 2011, though the underlying philosophy of the system has been maintained throughout. The system represents a deliberate attempt to get away from formalised court-based systems for dealing with both juvenile offenders and children who have been abused and neglected and it remains avowedly welfarist in its outlook.

There are a number of underlying philosophies within the system which reveal its character. First, and most importantly, it is assumed that children who have committed a criminal offence (the so-called "juvenile offender") ought to be treated in the same process as children who are being abused or neglected. The reason for this is that in both situations the system aims to get to the underlying problem facing the child rather than to respond to the events that have brought the child to the attention of the authorities. And it is a truth that is often denied, but remains the truth nevertheless, that the underlying problems are the same for both categories of children. These problems – low educational achievements, drug and alcohol abuse, domestic violence, parental unemployment, social exclusion – may be manifested through different children in different ways, but they are in essence the same.

Secondly, the system proceeds on the basis that a formal court setting and process may well be ideal to determine the facts upon which the child is brought within the system, but it is far from ideal in determining the appropriate response to the various problems facing the child and his or her family. So while disputes of fact may be resolved in a court of law, determining the disposal (that is to say, the response to these facts) is in the sole remit of a panel of trained but essentially lay persons – the children's hearing. Being drawn from a much wider section of the community than any bench of judges, or even sheriffs, the children's hearing can more readily be trusted to determine whether any particular style of upbringing of a child is simply not acceptable to general Scottish society today.

Thirdly, the system is almost exclusively welfare-based. In other words, the outcome in any particular case is determined by the children's hearing making its decisions on the basis of the welfare of the child. The hearing is not seeking to "punish" either the child or the parent or to make an order appropriate to the child's "offence" or to the parent's "badness". The aim is to see what is the best way forward for the child after it has been established that the upbringing of the child is, in some way, presently failing.

Fourthly, and following on from the third principle, the hearing system is designed to take a holistic view of the child and his or her whole environment. The finding that a specified "ground of referral" to the hearing applies in relation to a child opens that child's whole life to the examination of the children's hearing, so that the hearing can identify and address the circumstances within the family environment that led to the ground of concern. This is only proper since in the vast majority of cases to come before a children's hearing it is the family background to which the child's difficulties can be traced.

PROCESS AT A CHILDREN'S HEARING

The key figure in the process is an individual known as the children's reporter, or the reporter to the children's hearing. The first duty of the reporter is to receive information concerning the wellbeing of particular children. This information may come from a variety of sources, but will usually be from the police, schools or social services. It may come in addition from medical personnel, neighbours, friends, other family members and even (though this is virtually unknown) from the child himself or herself. The reporter must investigate the information he or she receives, and can ask for a report on the child from the social services and education departments of the local authority or the police. He or she must then make a decision as to (i) whether one or more of the specified grounds of concern listed in s 67 of the Children's Hearings (Scotland) Act 2011 are made out and (ii) whether a compulsory supervision order would benefit the child: if both decisions are affirmative, then the reporter must arrange a children's hearing to look at the child's case.

At the children's hearing, which is made up of three members of the children's panel (with at least one man and one woman), the chairing member will ask the child and the "relevant person" (that is to say, the parent of the child or other person significantly involved in the child's upbringing) whether or not they accept the accuracy of the grounds upon which the child has been referred to the hearing. These grounds, the "section 67 grounds", include that the child has been abused or neglected, has committed a criminal offence, has not been attending school, is beyond parental control, is living in an environment of domestic abuse, is indulging in risky behaviour, is at risk of being forced into marriage or is living with a child abuser or the victim of child abuse. If either the child or relevant person does not accept the accuracy of the stated ground, or does not understand it, the hearing has the choice of either discharging the referral or sending the matter to the sheriff court for proof – disputes as to the facts upon which the grounds of referral are based are matters for the sheriff and not for the hearing to resolve. But if the sheriff resolves the dispute by finding grounds established, the hearing will reconvene and must accept the facts as found by the sheriff. If the sheriff finds the grounds not established, the referral is discharged.

The purpose of the hearing itself (once grounds are accepted or established) is to discuss with the child and the relevant persons the grounds of concern and any other background information that might help the hearing to determine what the outcome should be. The aim is to find a solution that is in the best interests of the child and is most likely to resolve the problem that brought the child to the hearing. If the hearing decides that no further action is required then it will discharge the referral; otherwise it will impose a compulsory supervision order on the child. That order may be subject to such terms and conditions as the hearing thinks fit, and these terms and conditions clearly will differ depending upon the child's needs. It may be, in a care and protection case, that all the child needs is for his or her upbringing to be supervised by social workers, or that the child needs to be removed temporarily from dangerous and dirty home conditions. Rarely, the child may need to be removed with little expectation that he or she will return – but this would be an appropriate outcome only in the most extreme of circumstances when there is virtually no chance of the parents being able to change their way of life sufficiently to provide the child with the minimum standard of care. In a case where the child has committed an offence it may be that the terms of the compulsory supervision order oblige the child to attend group work to address offending behaviour, or (though this is rare) to meet his or her victim and to make practical reparation. Whatever the ground of referral, and not just in cases involving offences, the child may be required to reside at a children's home and it is possible to attach a condition that the child be locked up. Such an extreme outcome should never be seen in terms of "punishment", for that is not the purpose of the children's hearing system. But a child who is at risk of harming him or herself, or others, may well need the stability and control of secure accommodation before any work in addressing his or her life problems can begin.

There is of course an appeal procedure from decisions of the children's hearing, to the sheriff then the sheriff principal and then (or directly from the sheriff) to the Court of Session (but not thereafter to the Supreme Court). And any compulsory supervision order that has been imposed upon the child must be reviewed within a year, or earlier if requested by the local authority, the child or relevant person, or the hearing that originally imposed it. In any case, if not brought to an end at a review before then, the order will terminate on the child's 18th birthday.

ADOPTION ORDERS AND PERMANENCE ORDERS

Though the ultimate aim of all child protection measures that involved the removal of the child from his or her parents is to return that child to his or her home environment when it is safe to do so, it sometimes happens that there is no practical chance of this ever happening. It is unsatisfactory for a child to be kept subject to a compulsory supervision order for an indefinite number of years, because these orders are designed to be temporary, and it is disruptive for any child to be required to appear before hearings at least once a year: it is also unsettling for children to know that the hearing may continually rearrange their lives.

A children's hearing has no power to make permanent provision for keeping a child away from his or her parents (though it may facilitate plans to do so). Only a court can do so, by making either an adoption order or a permanence order under the Adoption and Children (Scotland) Act 2007. An adoption order, discussed in Chapter 2 above, is sometimes the end-result of the child protection process and, as we have seen, a parent who opposes the child's permanent removal must have his or her consent to adoption dispensed with. This will usually be on the basis that the parent is unable satisfactorily to fulfil parental responsibilities but even when that cannot be shown the parent's consent may be dispensed with if the child's welfare requires this. "Requires" imports an imperative, a situation in which nothing less than adoption will suffice, and it is not enough simply to show that the child would be better off with prospective adopters than with his or her own parents.

The effect of an adoption order is to sever completely the parent–child relationship and sometimes (especially with older children) their needs require that they be removed permanently from their parents' care but do *not* require that the parents be cut out of their lives completely. Children have a capacity to love parents even when these parents are unable or unfit to bring them up, and children may benefit from a continued (if distant) connection with their family roots. For such children, an adoption order is inappropriate but a permanence order may be made instead by the court: this order has the effect of making permanent provision for the child's upbringing away from his or her parents – sharing parental responsibilities and parental rights between the local authority and the people actually caring for the child – but not destroying the existing parent–child relationship. A permanence order may be made in two circumstances: where there is no person who has the right to have the child living with him or her or otherwise to regulate the child's residence, or where there is such a person but the child's residence with that person would be likely to be seriously detrimental to the welfare of the child. If these conditions are satisfied then it is open to the court to make a permanence order, but it may do so only when it considers that it would be better for the child that the order be made than that it should not be made, and the court must regard the need to safeguard and promote the welfare of the child, throughout childhood, as the paramount consideration.

All permanence orders will contain what is called the "mandatory provision", which vests in the local authority the right to determine where the child is to live. The permanence order may also contain "ancillary provisions", which will typically allocate parental responsibilities and parental rights between the local authority and the child's carers, or make provision for contact between the child and his or her parents. The order may also include a provision granting authority for the child to be adopted, so long as the court is satisfied that it is likely that the child will be placed for adoption. If such a provision is to be included the parent must consent to the provision, or have his or her consent thereto dispensed with on the same grounds as consent to an adoption order may be dispensed with. Thereafter, the parent's consent to the subsequent adoption order is not needed.

EMERGENCY PROTECTION

It sometimes happens that a local authority is of the view that a child needs to be removed from his or her home environment even before a children's hearing has had a chance to consider the case fully and properly. This will be the case whenever it is of the view that the child is at risk of serious harm unless action is taken immediately. In these circumstances the local authority can apply to the sheriff for a "child protection order" (ss 38 and 39 of the 2011 Act) which, if granted, lasts a maximum of eight working days. During that time, while the child is kept away from his or her family, the reporter will draw up grounds of referral and the children's hearing that has to be held on the eighth working day after the removal of the child will consider the child's case. If the eighth working day hearing cannot at that stage make a final decision (for example because the grounds of referral have been denied) and the child continues to require to be kept away from home, this may be done by means of an interim compulsory supervision order.

Police officers also have the power to remove a child summarily from a source of imminent danger but their power lasts for only twenty-four hours: during this time the local authority will be contacted and it is for them to decide whether to seek a child protection order (and thereafter for the reporter to decide whether to arrange a children's hearing).

CHILD PROTECTION AND THE EUROPEAN CONVENTION ON HUMAN RIGHTS

Removing a child from his or her parents, or even interfering in the upbringing of a child by means of a compulsory supervision order under which the child remains at home, is, necessarily, an interference with both the child's and the parents' right to private and family life, respect for which is guaranteed by Art 8(1) of the European Convention on Human Rights (ECHR). It follows that any such interference must be justified by Art 8(2), that is to say must be shown to be "necessary in a democratic society". What this means is that the aim of the interference must be in accordance with the law, follow a legitimate aim (which is easy to establish since protection of children is not only legitimate but a state obligation) and be "proportionate" to that aim, or no more severe than is necessary to achieve the identified legitimate aim. The proportionality test finds reflection in ss 28 and 29 of the 2011 Act, under which the hearing and the court may make orders over the child only when it would be better for the child that the order be in force than not. It has been held on numerous occasions by the European Court of Human Rights that the aim of state intervention must have as its ultimate goal family reunification, and that any decision to have a child permanently removed from his or her parents can be justified only in the most extreme of circumstances. But that Court does recognise that in some cases family reunification will simply not be possible and that a child's interests may very occasionally require a complete cessation of family life with his or her existing family (justifying an adoption order or a permanence order). In addition to proportionality, the two most important issues relating to European Convention on Human Rights compatibility are (i) ensuring full participation in the decision-making process by both the child and the child's parents (or anyone else whose family life with the child is threatened by the state intervention); and (ii) the requirement on local authorities to maintain contact between a child removed from home and his or her family, wherever possible.

Essential Facts

- The children's hearing system is based on the belief that children who offend are as much in need of care and protection as children who have been offended against.
- The children's hearing determines what is in the interests of the child, but the court determines whether the specified ground of concern, in respect of which the child was referred to a hearing, exists or not (if the matter is disputed or the child or relevant person does not understand the ground).
- Once the grounds of referral have been established, the hearing may take into account any other facts that are relevant to the child's welfare.
- A permanence order is a sub-adoption order allowing the child to be kept away from his or her parents permanently, but not breaking the legal parent–child relationship (as an adoption order does).
- A permanence order contains the mandatory provision granting the local authority the right to determine where the child is to live, ancillary provisions allocating parental responsibilities and parental rights, and sometimes a provision granting authority for the child to be adopted.
- A child protection order may be granted by a sheriff to provide immediate protection to a child in an emergency: this will permit the summary removal of the child and the keeping of the child in a place of safety for eight working days.
- Removal of a child from his or her home, or any other state intervention in the upbringing process, is an infringement of Art 8(1) of the European Convention on Human Rights, and it therefore requires justification under Art 8(2) as being a proportionate response to the risks facing the child.
- The ultimate aim of all child care proceedings should be to return the child to his or her family and in the meantime contact between parent and child should, wherever possible, be encouraged.

Essential Statutes

Children and Young Persons (Scotland) Act 1937

Section 12 makes it a crime for anyone over the age of 16 to ill-treat, neglect, abandon or expose a child, in a manner likely to cause the child unnecessary suffering or injury to health.

Matrimonial Homes (Family Protection) (Scotland) Act 1981

Section 4 allows the court to exclude a person from his or her home, on the application of their partner, if this is necessary to protect that person or any child of the family from conduct or threatened or reasonably apprehended conduct which is or would be injurious to the physical or mental health of the applicant or the child.

Antisocial Behaviour etc (Scotland) Act 2004

Section 102 allows the court to make a parenting order on the application of the local authority or of the children's reporter if the child has engaged in antisocial behaviour. Section 103 provides that the effect of a parenting order is to require the person specified in the order to comply with such requirements as the order contains.

Adoption and Children (Scotland) Act 2007

Sections 29 and 30 allow an adoption order to be made when sought by individuals or couples (as there defined). Section 31 provides that an adoption order may not be made except with the consent of each of the child's parents and guardians, and it sets out the circumstances in which parental consent may be dispensed with. Section 80 allows the court to make a permanence order, on application of a local authority, containing the mandatory provision, any ancillary provisions and if other specified requirements are satisfied authority for the child to be adopted. Section 81 defines the mandatory provision as one that vests in the local authority the right to regulate the child's residence and the responsibility to provide the child with guidance. Section 82 defines ancillary provisions as those that allocate parental responsibilities and parental rights between the local authority, the parents and those who are bringing up the child. Section 84 provides that a permanence order may be made only when either there is no person with the right to regulate the child's residence, or there is such a person but for the child to reside with that person would be likely to be seriously detrimental to the welfare of the child.

Children's Hearings (Scotland) Act 2011

Section 25 ensures that the welfare of the child is the paramount consideration of the court or children's hearing in making any of the orders under the 2011 Act. Section 27 requires the court and children's hearing to have regard to any views that the child wishes to express, though this does not apply when a sheriff is deciding whether to make a child protection order. Sections 38 and 39 allow the court to make a child protection order if there is suspected or believed to be some danger imminently facing the child. Section 67 sets out the grounds upon which a child may be referred to a children's hearing. Sections 91 and 119 allow the children's hearing to make a compulsory supervision order whenever (once section 67 grounds have been accepted or established) it considers this is necessary for the protection, guidance, treatment or control of the child.

Essential Cases

O v Rae (1993): four children were referred to a children's hearing on the basis of lack of parental care, and supervision requirements (which are now called compulsory supervision orders) were made over the four children, requiring them to live in residential accommodation away from their father. At a review of this requirement the social background report referred to an allegation that the father had sexually abused the eldest child and the hearing decided to continue the supervision requirement. The father appealed on the ground that the allegation had never been tested in evidence and so it ought not to have been allowed to influence the decision of the hearing.

The Court of Session held that the hearing had been correct to take into account allegations made in a social background report, even when these facts were denied and had not been tested in evidence. All that is required to be proved in evidence are the facts making up the grounds of referral, and the outcome of any case can be determined by other facts since the hearing is able to look at all the circumstances of the case, including those circumstances denied by one or more of the parties.

S v Miller (2001): a child was referred to the children's hearing on account of his involvement in a violent incident with numerous individuals, which led to the death of his father. The hearing authorised his detention in secure accommodation. The child challenged the procedure as being contrary to Art 6 of the European Convention on Human Rights since he had not been allowed paid legal representation at the hearing.

The court held that a blanket ban on legal aid for representation of children at hearings was not compatible with the ECHR. (Legal aid was made available to both child and relevant person by the Children's Hearings (Scotland) Act 2011.)

Re B (A Child) (2013): A 3-year-old child had been removed from her parents shortly after birth but contact had gone well since. The parents were able to care for the child adequately, but they had very severe difficulties in dealing with authority (of any nature) – they were compulsive liars and fantasists and constantly raised spurious complaints. If the child were returned to their care, she would be loved and adequately looked after, but would be given disastrous attitudes which would spoil her life. Was the threshold for permanent removal of this child from these parents met? Was there a "likelihood of significant harm" befalling the child?

The Supreme Court (by four men to one woman) held that the threshold had been met and the child had to be kept from the parents. Impairment of emotional development was included in the concept of harm. "Likelihood" and "significant" operated as a matrix and the less likelihood of harm, the more significant it would have to be, and vice versa. Quoted with approval was the following statement of Hedley J in *Re L (Care: Threshold Criteria)* [2007] 1 FLR 2050 at 2063:

Society must be willing to tolerate very diverse standards of parenting, including the eccentric, the barely adequate and the inconsistent. It follows too that children will inevitably have both very different experiences of parenting and very unequal consequences flowing from it. It means that some children will experience disadvantage and harm, while others flourish in atmospheres of loving security and emotional stability. These are the consequences of our fallible humanity and it is not the province of the state to spare children all the consequences of defective parenting. In any event, it simply could not be done.

The present child, however, was spared the consequences of defective parenting.

Johansen v Norway (1997): a baby was removed from her mother on birth and placed with foster carers. The mother was inadequate, did not look after herself or her children, was addicted to anti-depressants, was starving herself and had been in a series of violent relationships; she was mentally unstable.

The European Court held that the decision to remove the baby was not contrary to Art 8 of the ECHR, but that the decision by the authorities to prevent any access between mother and child was a breach. Removal was a proportionate response to the difficulties but refusing access made it increasingly difficult to work towards the reintegration of the child with the mother, which should be the ultimate aim of all child protection processes.

E v United Kingdom (2003): serious physical and sexual abuse had been committed against a family of children by their mother's cohabitant. Though he was eventually convicted and imprisoned, the issue of abuse had never been raised at children's hearings, with the result that no effective protection had ever been given to the children. The children then sued the UK Government for not acting to protect them, claiming a breach of Art 3 of the European Convention on Human Rights (the right to be free from torture or inhuman or degrading treatment).

The European Court held that there was a breach because, in the circumstances of the case, the local authority ought to have been aware of the cohabitant's history of sexual abuse and of his close contact with the vulnerable children in this family.

Haase v Germany (2005): Mrs Haase had twelve children and she and her husband brought them up in a harsh, repressive and inconsistent manner. The German state eventually stepped in for the good of the children and removed the seven younger ones, including a new-born baby.

The European Court held that this amounted to an infringement of the parents' Art 8 right to family life. There had been no imminent danger to the children and the parents had not been sufficiently involved in the decision-making process. Also, the removal of a new-born baby from its mother was an exceptionally harsh action that required extremely strong reasons to justify it, which did not exist in the present case. In addition, it is never sufficient on its own to remove a child from its family just because it would be better off elsewhere.

S v L (2012): a child was removed from its mother who was addicted to drugs. While the child was being looked after, the mother recovered and wanted to resume the care of her child, but an adoption application was made. The mother refused to consent to that adoption and her consent would have to be dispensed with. The ground of parental incapacity was not available since the mother was no longer a drug addict and so the petitioners sought to have her consent dispensed with on the ground that the child's welfare "otherwise requires". The mother argued that this ground for dispensation was contrary to Art 8 of the European Convention on Human Rights since the child's welfare was too amorphous a concept to justify the permanent removal of a child from its parent.

The Supreme Court held that the welfare ground for dispensing with parental consent in the Adoption and Children (Scotland) Act 2007 was not contrary to the ECHR, since welfare had to "require" the child's adoption. That word imports an imperative into the decision and the ground cannot be used, therefore, unless nothing less than adoption will suffice to secure the child's welfare. If that is the case, then the parent's consent can be dispensed with, even when the parent is capable of bringing up the child adequately.

6 MARRIAGE AND CIVIL PARTNERSHIP

The conjugal relationships that adults enter into are governed by the law on two different levels, depending upon the formality of the relationship. By "conjugal relationships" is meant here domestic relationships entered into voluntarily by two individuals combining their social, emotional and financial lives together. They are relationships which start out as, or develop into (but do not necessarily remain), sexual. Though not entirely accurate (as we will see) it is convenient to classify conjugal relations into a binary model, with those that are registered with the state (as either marriage or civil partnership) being compared with those that are not so registered. Marriage is the registered relationship of either an opposite-sex or a same-sex couple; civil partnership is an alternative form of registered relationship for same-sex couples, but it has virtually the same effects as marriage. Unregistered relationships ("cohabiting couples") are examined in the next chapter.

ENTERING INTO REGISTERED RELATIONSHIPS

The statutory means of entering into both marriage and civil partnership are largely but not completely the same: they are set out in the Marriage (Scotland) Act 1977 and the Civil Partnership Act 2004 respectively. The parties must give notice to the district registrar of their intention to marry or enter into a civil partnership, and so long as the district registrar is satisfied of the parties' capacity or eligibility to do so the district registrar will issue a schedule which gives permission to proceed. In religious or belief marriages or civil partnerships functionaries from the relevant organisation have the power, once in possession of this schedule, to conduct the actual ceremony on behalf of the state; with civil marriages and civil registration of civil partnerships the ceremony is conducted and controlled by the registrar (who retains the marriage or civil partnership schedule). In either case the ceremony must be witnessed by two witnesses professing to be (in the case of marriage) and actually being (in the case of civil partnership) over 16 years of age; the parties must agree to be the other's spouse or civil partner; and after the ceremony the schedule must be registered with the district registrar. It is left largely to the parties, in negotiation with the celebrant (the functionary from a relevant organisation or the district registrar), what form the ceremony itself is to take and where it may take place.

For marriage (though not for civil partnerships) the common law permitted parties to enter into this legal institution even without any formal ceremony and without, therefore, registration of the entering into the relationship. Of the three informal methods permitted by the common law, only one survived the statutory modernisation of Scottish marriage law in the Marriage (Scotland) Act 1939, and that remaining method has not been able to be used since 2006 – though marriages contracted before then may still be declared valid after that date. This informal method of getting married is known as marriage by cohabitation with habit and repute. The cohabitation must be for a significant length of time (so long as at least some of it takes place before the commencement of the abolishing Family Law (Scotland) Act 2006). The court has accepted periods of just short of a year. The cohabitation must have taken place at a time when the parties were, in law, free to marry each other. The "habit and repute", that is to say the understanding of outsiders that the couple are married, must be general and widely held but the doctrine is not avoided by showing that a small number of people knew the truth. So a couple whom most of their friends and neighbours thought were married but whose parents, say, knew had never gone through a ceremony of marriage, might well be considered to be married by the law. To establish marriage by this means it is necessary to raise an action for declarator of marriage. This by-product of an earlier age has long outlived its usefulness and was latterly simply a means by which cohabitants could gain legal rights on death or separation otherwise denied them (by pretending to be married and accessing thereby the benefits of marriage). The typical case was when one cohabitant died and the other had no right to succeed to any part of the deceased's estate – unless she could establish that she had been married to the deceased. There was, of course, no registration of this form of marriage, though the court decree will be proof positive whenever it is needed.

As a common law doctrine, designed to provide a route for entry into the common law institution of marriage, there was no equivalent for civil partnership which is a statutory creation. And while the Marriage and Civil Partnership (Scotland) Act 2014 extends the principle (insofar as it continues to exist) to marriages involving same-sex couples (who were not, of course, eligible to marry each other at common law), it does not extend it to civil partnerships.

CONSEQUENCES OF MARRIAGE AND CIVIL PARTNERSHIP

Marriage and civil partnership create a status, by which is meant that they attract rights and obligations irrespective of the factual state of the relationship, and this is so not only between the parties *inter se* but also between each individual party and the rest of the world. The major consequences in law are as follows.

Aliment

Each partner to a marriage or civil partnership is obliged to aliment the other. By this is meant that each partner must provide for the financial support of the other and, if that support is not forthcoming, each may sue the other. The rules of aliment are contained in sections 1 to 7 of the Family Law (Scotland) Act 1985. Aliment is a statutory obligation based upon the status of marriage or civil partnership and it follows that the right to aliment terminates as soon as the marriage or civil partnership comes to an end whether on death or on divorce (though in either case the claimant may seek a part of the other's property).

Succession

Spouses and civil partners cannot be disinherited. This has long been the common law rule with spouses, and it is statutorily so for civil partners. The primary entitlement is known as legal rights, whereby the spouse or civil partner is entitled to one third of his or her deceased partner's moveable estate (if the partner is also survived by issue, that is to say children or grandchildren or great grandchildren etc) or one half of the moveable estate (if the deceased is not survived by any children etc). This entitlement is not in addition to any legacy that the deceased may have left his or her partner and so if there is a legacy in a will the survivor must choose to accept either the legacy or his or her legal rights. Another entitlement, this time statutory for both spouses and civil partners, is known as prior rights. These are paid only when the deceased dies intestate or partially intestate (that is to say, without an effectual will). There are rights to cash, to the family home and to the furnishings and plenishings of the family home (in each case up to stated financial limits). The rules for both spouses and civil partners are contained in ss 8 and 9 of the Succession (Scotland) Act 1964. Finally, if the deceased's estate has anything left over after the payment of legal rights and prior rights, the spouse or civil partner has a claim to the free estate that is not otherwise distributed according to a will (because either the deceased did not make a will or the will was not valid or the will did not cover all the property owned by the deceased). This right to the free estate is, however, post-poned to the preferred free estate claims of the deceased's descendants, parent and siblings. Of course it is open to one partner in a registered relationship, whether marriage or civil partnership, to make a will leaving all his or her property to the other partner (though if he or she does so but also leaves issue, the partner takes only after payment of the legal rights claimed by such issue).

Right to occupy the family home

One of the most important rights that is granted to all spouses and civil partners is the right to occupy the family home even when that home is owned exclusively by one only. This right was conferred by the Matrimonial Homes (Family Protection) (Scotland) Act 1981 and replicated for civil partners by the Civil Partnership Act 2004. It was previously relatively common for the family home to be owned only by one party – usually the husband – and in that situation before the 1981 Act the wife had neither legal title to the house nor legal right to live there: she lived in the family home on the husband's sufferance. Of course, she had a remedy of divorce if the husband excluded her but she remained homeless in these circumstances. So the 1981 Act conferred on what is called the "non-entitled spouse" (or, under the Civil Partnership Act 2004, "non-entitled partner") the right to occupy the family home to which he or she has no legal title of ownership. This right is good against third parties, so that it cannot be defeated by the owner of the house selling it on. The right lasts as long as the marriage or civil partnership lasts, so that at its termination (whether on death, divorce or dissolution) the right comes to an end. But death brings succession rights and divorce or dissolution brings rights to claim financial provision. If both the spouses or both the civil partners have joint title to the family home (as is much more common today) then property law rather than the 1981 Act gives both the right to occupy in any case.

Protection from domestic violence

The rules here are mostly contained in the Matrimonial Homes (Family Protection) (Scotland) Act 1981, and replicated in the Civil Partnership Act 2004. These Acts provide that a spouse (or civil partner) can seek an exclusion order excluding his or her partner from the family home if this is necessary to protect him or herself or any child of the family from any conduct or threatened or reasonably apprehended conduct of the other partner. On the same test a spouse or civil partner can seek an interdict against the partner. It used to be more significant that the interdict was granted under the 1981 Act since attached thereto could be a power of arrest, authorising the police to arrest a partner who breached the interdict – a power not otherwise attachable to interdicts which were seen very much as civil law remedies. Now, however, the Protection from Abuse (Scotland) Act 2001 allows the court to attach a power of arrest to any interdict designed to protect against personal violence and so the availability of an interdict under the 1981 Act or the 2004 Act is far less important today. The Domestic Abuse (Scotland) Act 2011 makes it a criminal offence to breach a domestic abuse interdict to which a power of arrest is attached.

Tax

There are various tax consequences of a person acquiring the status of married person or civil partner. This book is not the place to explore all the taxation legislation, but the most important consequence may usefully be mentioned here. This relates to inheritance tax. Under the Inheritance Tax Act 1984, as amended, if a person dies owning property above a certain value, the transfer of that property to his or her successors will generate a liability to taxation. Importantly, however, transfers to spouses or civil partners are exempt from this tax. The state takes the view that if property passes on the death of one partner to the other there is little lost to the public purse since on the death of the other their (now joint) estates will attract the tax liability; conversely it would be inequitable for a spouse or civil partner who inherits the estate of his or her deceased partner to be forced to sell part of that estate in order to pay the taxation due. That would typically be the most valuable part of the estate, the house, which would result in the survivor losing his or her home. Thus the exemption.

Debts and bankruptcy

If one spouse or civil partner becomes bankrupt, the creditors are entitled to challenge any transfers the bankrupt person made to his or her domestic partner in the past five years (Bankruptcy (Scotland) Act 1985). If the family home is threatened with sale by the creditors, the non-entitled spouse or civil partner must be kept informed. Any domestic partner who has acted as the other's cautioner (that is to say, guarantor for debts) can escape that obligation by showing that undue pressure was brought on him or her to act as such: if the creditor is aware of the relationship he or she is put on notice to ensure that undue pressure was not in fact brought to bear.

Relationships with children

The fact that the parents of children are not and never have been married to each other used to have devastating consequences for the child. This was the old concept of "illegitimacy". Today, the effects in law of "illegitimacy" are limited to entitlement to succeed to titles of honour like dukedoms, baronetcies, coats of arms and the Crown. But there remain some crucial differences in terms of the legal responsibilities and legal rights that fathers have. For one thing, marriage creates a presumption of paternity. In other words, if a child is born to a married woman, her husband is presumed to be the father of the child. Additionally, if a father is married to the mother of his child, he acquires by that marriage (rather than by registration as father) parental responsibilities and parental rights in relation to the child. These rules do not apply to civil partnership which, being same-sex relationships only, will never lead to children with both partners being the genetic parent. (Civil partners can, of course, adopt, and become parents by means discussed in Chapter 2 above).

Criminal law

The criminal law is affected in a number of ways by the fact that parties have married or entered into a civil partnership. First and (perhaps) most obviously, if a married or civilly empartnered individual goes through a form of marriage or civil partnership before the end of the existing legal relationship then the new marriage or civil partnership has no effect in law. Doing so amounted to the common law crime of bigamy (if involving a marriage and a later purported marriage); today for both marriage and civil partnership it is a statutory offence to enter a marriage or civil partnership while already married to, or in a civil partnership with, another person (Marriage and Civil Partnership (Scotland) Act 2014, s 28, amending s 24 of the Marriage (Scotland) Act 1977). This crime was originally designed to protect parties from fraudulent marriages, but the rule is probably today better understood as designed to avoid frauds on the public register since marriage and civil partnership result in the conferral of a variety of civic benefits on the parties thereto. Another consequence in the criminal law concerns the law of incest and related offences, which is governed by the Criminal Law (Consolidation) (Scotland) Act 1995. It is the crime of incest to have sexual intercourse with various members of one's genetic family. It is also an offence to have sexual intercourse with some of the relations of one's spouse or civil partner. So not only is it a crime to have sexual intercourse with one's own child but it is also a crime to have sexual intercourse with one's step-child (that is to say, the child of one's spouse or civil partner): it is not automatically a crime to have sexual intercourse with one's unregistered partner's child, but it might be if it involves an abuse of a position of trust as defined by the Sexual Offences (Scotland) Act 2009.

Miscellaneous effects

Marriage and civil partnership have a number of other effects in law. Some apply to cohabitation too: first, the rule in s 25 of the Family Law (Scotland) Act 1985 that in a question as to the ownership of any household goods (as defined in s 25(3)) it is presumed (rebuttably) that the goods in question are owned in common; secondly, the rule in s 26 of the 1985 Act that any savings from a housekeeping allowance that one makes to the other are jointly owned; and thirdly, on the negligently caused death of one of the spouses or civil partners the other is entitled to damages under the Damages (Scotland) Act 2011 for his or her loss of support and for a non-patrimonial amount designed to reflect the distress and anxiety endured by the survivor in contemplation of the suffering of the deceased, grief and sorrow, and any non-patrimonial benefit of the deceased's society and guidance, now lost. A few other consequences of marriage and civil partnership do not apply to cohabitants, including the rules on nationality and immigration, and the fact that spouses and civil partners are entitled to refuse to give evidence that will incriminate their partner who is the accused in a criminal court case.

Essential Facts

- Marriage is for either opposite-sex or same-sex couples while civil partnership (presently, at least) is limited to same-sex couples, having been designed in 2004 as a bridge between no recognition of same-sex couples and full marital recognition.
- Marriage by cohabitation with habit and repute requires that at least some cohabitation between the parties occurred before the Family Law (Scotland) Act 2006 came into force.
- Marriages and civil partnerships must be celebrated and registered in the presence of both parties and two witnesses, and both parties must give free consent.
- Both marriage and civil partnership ceremonies may be conducted either by a district registrar ("civil marriage" or "civil registration of civil partnership") or by an official of a religious or belief organisation ("religious or belief marriage" or "religious or belief civil partnership").

- For religious or belief marriages or civil partnerships, both officials and the religious or belief organisations to which they belong must be specifically registered as being willing to conduct marriage or civil partnership ceremonies for same-sex couples, and it is no breach of the equality legislation for them to refuse to be so registered, or to seek registration only in respect of opposite-sex couples. District registrars, being state officials, cannot however refuse to conduct civil same-sex marriage or civil registration of civil partnerships.
- The major consequences of marriage and civil partnership are alimentary obligations, succession rights, occupancy rights in the family home, extra protection from domestic violence and exemption from inheritance tax.

Essential Statutes

Succession (Scotland) Act 1964

Sections 8 and 9 make provision for a surviving spouse or civil partner to receive prior rights in succession on the death of his or her spouse or civil partner.

Marriage (Scotland) Act 1977

Section 3 provides that a marriage notice must be submitted to the district registrar, specifying the parties to the marriage, and where and when it will be solemnised. Section 5 sets out the objections that may be made to a proposed marriage and requires the district registrar (where the objection is minor) or the Registrar General (where the objection is to the essential validity of the marriage) to investigate and, if the major objection is good, requires the district registrar to prevent the marriage taking place. Section 6 requires the district registrar to issue a marriage schedule, being the celebrant's authorisation to solemnise the marriage. Sections 8 to 12 set out who may solemnise a marriage; if the marriage is to be between a couple of the same sex the celebrant, and the celebrant's organisation, must be registered as willing to conduct such marriages.

Matrimonial Homes (Family Protection) (Scotland) Act 1981

Section 1 provides that where the family home is owned by only one spouse, the other spouse has a right to occupy that home. Section 6 ensures that the right of occupancy cannot be defeated by the owning spouse disposing of the property.

Civil Partnership (Scotland) Act 2004

Sections 88–94 replicate for civil partnerships the provisions in the Marriage (Scotland) Act 1977. Sections 101 and 106 replicate for civil partners the provisions in the Matrimonial Homes (Family Protection) (Scotland) Act 1981 applicable to spouses. Section 131 replicates for surviving civil partners the common law rule conferring legal rights in succession on surviving spouses.

Family Law (Scotland) Act 2006

Section 3 abolishes marriage by cohabitation with habit and repute, except where the parties entered a purported marriage abroad which turned out to be invalid, and one of the parties has now died domiciled in Scotland, not knowing that the marriage was invalid.

Damages (Scotland) Act 2011

Section 4 provides that a person who negligently caused the death of a member of the pursuer's immediate family is liable to pay the survivor a sum to compensate for loss of support, distress and anxiety at the deceased's suffering, grief and sorrow at the relative's death, and for loss of non-patrimonial benefit derived from the deceased's society. Section 14 defines "immediate family" to include the spouse and civil partner of the deceased.

Marriage and Civil Partnership (Scotland) Act 2014

Section 4 amends the definition of marriage so that it means marriage between persons of different sexes and marriage between persons of the same sex. Sections 8–11 allow parties in a civil partnership to convert that relationship into a marriage. Section 28 abolishes the common law crime of bigamy and creates in its place the statutory offence of any person in a marriage or civil partnership entering into a marriage or civil partnership.

Essential Cases

Hyde v Hyde (1866): Hyde was an Englishman who travelled extensively in North America. He married his wife in the territory of Utah, before that part of North America entered the United States of America. It was assumed that Utah law permitted polygamy, as the Mormon faith then did (and the Fundamentalist schismatics still do): Hyde married his wife according to the rituals of the Mormons. He subsequently left both the Mormon faith and his wife, and she took another husband, a course of action allowed by her faith.

Hyde, by now back in England, sought to bring his marriage to an end by divorce, on the basis of his wife's adultery. The judge, Lord Penzance, refused to grant the divorce, on the basis that there was no marriage as English law understood the concept and therefore there was nothing to bring to an end.

Lord Penzance laid down what has come to be regarded as the common law definition of marriage: "Marriage is the voluntary union for life of one man and one woman to the exclusion of all others." He spoke at a time less than ten years after the introduction of judicial divorce into England (though Scotland has had divorce since the Reformation).

Wetherhill v Sheikh (2005): Karen Wetherhill fell in love with Zahid Sheikh, even though he was already married to someone else. But that was an arranged marriage to which Zahid was not committed, and so Karen and Zahid moved in together, started a business together and had two children together. Zahid's parents, with whom his (actual) wife lived, would accept Karen as a member of the family only if she were married to Zahid, so they told his parents that they were indeed married (the parents' faith having no problem with polygamy). The (actual) wife left Scotland and soon thereafter divorced Zahid. Karen was now free to marry the father of her children, but she refused to do so, fearing enveilment. Zahid's family continued to believe they were already married in any case. The relationship broke down some years later and Karen sought a declarator that they were married by cohabitation with habit and repute so that she could get financial provision on divorce. (Remember, she had refused to marry Zahid.)

The court held that they were married. They had lived together for twelve years and Lord Philip found that there was sufficient habit and repute. This case may have been the nail in the coffin that finally persuaded our law-makers to do away with the mischievous doctrine of marriage by cohabitation with habit and repute.

Saleh v Saleh (1987): Carol Mackie agreed to marry Abdallah Saleh and they submitted a marriage notice in Grangemouth where it was put on public display. In fact, however, the marriage took place in Edinburgh (at that city's mosque) where there had been no notice. The relationship broke down and Carol sought a declarator of nullity. However, no marriage schedule had been drawn up to authorise the mosque officials to conduct a lawful marriage and the marriage was never registered. The court agreed with the Lord Advocate that while s 23A of the Marriage (Scotland) Act 1977 allowed errors as to the place of the ceremony to be ignored, that section could not save a marriage where the marriage schedule had never been registered.

Smith v Bank of Scotland (1997): Mrs Smith was persuaded by her husband to act as cautioner for her husband (that is to say, guarantor for his debts), with the family home being used as a security. The husband reneged on his debts and, unless Mrs Smith could escape the cautionary obligation, the family home would be lost. She proved that her husband had deceived her as to the nature of the cautionary obligation.

The House of Lords held that since the creditor knew of the relationship between the debtor (Mr Smith) and the cautioner (Mrs Smith) they could be taken to be aware of the risk that the one had unduly influenced the other and so the creditor could not enforce the security unless it had taken steps to warn the cautioner of the risks and advised her to take independent legal advice. Mrs Smith was not so warned or advised, therefore the creditor was in bad faith and so unable to enforce the security. Mrs Smith kept her home (and Mr Smith avoided paying his debts).

Goodridge v Massachusetts (2003): the constitution of Massachusetts has a strong anti-discrimination clause and a number of same-sex couples sought to use that clause to have declared invalid the common law rule that marriage is restricted to relationships between a man and a woman. The onus was on the state to provide rational justification to exclude same-sex couples from the rights and responsibilities of marriage.

The court held that the state had not discharged its onus of providing such a rational justification and that therefore the state was obliged to amend its law to permit same-sex couples to marry. The state went back to the court and asked, "Do you mean we have to let same-sex couples *marry*? Can't we just let them enter into civil unions?" The court answered "Yes" and "No" respectively. Marriage has a symbolic importance beyond its actual legal consequences and so a civil partnership regime which gave the same legal consequences as marriage but withheld the social status inherent in the name "marriage" fell short of the equality demanded by the constitution.

Burden v United Kingdom (2008): two spinster sisters who lived together claimed that they were being discriminated against by the inheritance tax rule that exempted spouses and civil partners, but not cohabiting sisters, from inheritance tax. The European Court rejected their claim. A state's tax regime was within its margin of appreciation and in any case it was rational to treat relationships sanctioned and regulated by the law, and in which the parties had made a public declaration of mutual support, differently from informal and voluntary relationships such as that between siblings who choose to live together.

Ladele v United Kingdom (2013): Ladele was a district registrar whose duties included conducting civil marriage ceremonies. When the Civil Partnership Act 2004 came into force she refused to conduct civil partnership ceremonies and when her employers refused to accommodate her objections she felt obliged to resign, which she claimed was constructive dismissal. She lost in the UK courts and took the UK Government to Strasbourg, arguing that her right under Art 9 of the European Convention on Human Rights (right to freedom of thought, conscience and religion) had been infringed.

The European Court rejected her claim holding that the failure to provide a conscientious objection clause for public officials was not contrary to Art 9 since the state had an obligation to provide all its services in a non-discriminatory manner. If the public official could not reconcile the law to his or her own religious convictions he or she was free to seek another job and so the right to religious freedom was not interfered with.

7 UNREGISTERED COUPLES

Of course, not all couples who live together in a conjugal relationship want to register that relationship with the state. An increasing number of couples who are technically "unmarried" and are not registered as "civil partners" nevertheless lead their lives in a way that is, to all intents and purposes, indistinguishable from that led by those couples who are registered with the state. Such couples are called "cohabiting couples" and the parties thereto should be referred to as "cohabitants" (and not, as is common, "cohabitees"). Since most of the consequences of marriage and civil partnership discussed above are conferred in recognition of the status conferred by the state as a result of the couple publicly undertaking mutual obligations to each other, it is right and proper that they are not extended to cohabitants – who have not made any such public undertaking. Many people eschew the very concept of marriage or civil partnership; some prefer to regulate the consequences of their own relationships without the state telling them what these consequences are to be; and a good few people who have been married and did not like the legal consequences thereof (or perhaps did not like the legal and financial consequences of divorce or dissolution) prefer now to enter into domestic relationships over which they have more personal control. In these circumstances it is perfectly justifiable for the law not to impose the full gamut of marital consequences, and this does not amount to discrimination against unregistered couples. For many the choice is theirs and if they want all the legal consequences described in the previous chapter to apply to their relationship then they are free to register it as a marriage or civil partnership. Of course some couples cannot register, for example because they are not free to marry or enter into a civil partnership, but that too is not discrimination, for that lack of freedom is nearly always justified by good social policy, such as preventing child marriages or bigamous marriages.

There are, however, a number of consequences, mostly of a protective nature, that the law does give to couples who are cohabitants. Before examining these consequences, however, it is important to be aware of how the law defines cohabitation.

THE MEANING OF "COHABITATION" AND "COHABITANT"

The consequences about to be discussed are virtually all contained within the terms of particular Acts and it follows that the couples covered by the statute will be defined by the statute itself. They all use phrases like "living together as husband and wife" and (before same-sex couples were able to marry) "living together as if they were civil partners", and that is generally as far as the law goes in identifying when a couple will become a cohabiting couple. There are two main elements here. First, the couple must "live together": that is the literal meaning of "cohabitation". It is to be noted, in this context, that it is no part of the definition of marriage or civil partnership that the registered partners live together. It is not unknown (and particularly so in the lesbian and gay community) for couples who see themselves as conjugal "couples" to retain separate houses and to live apart. If they do they are not "cohabitants" in the eyes of the law. Secondly, the relationship must be characterised by the elements that are common for married couples (including, of course, same-sex married couples). The unregistered couple must share their lives together in the way that is traditional for registered couples, that is to say must share mutual interests, share a social life, be economically interdependent and be regarded as a member of the other's wider family. As the marital relationship is a relationship based upon sex, so living together as if married requires that the couple's relationship be, or at least have been at an earlier stage, sexually intimate. Many statutes explicitly extend the phrase "living together as husband and wife" to same-sex couples (who, literally, cannot live together as husband and wife because these words are gendered); and the Marriage and Civil Partnership (Scotland) Act 2014 now explicitly provides that the phrase, wherever it appears in statute, is to include two people of the same sex who are living together as if they were married to each other.

MINOR LEGAL CONSEQUENCES OF COHABITATION

There are a number of fairly minor legal consequences of a couple whose relationship is unregistered but who are living together as if they were married, and they have applied for many years. In addition, since 2006, there have been two major legal consequences. The minor consequences are as follows:

(1) Occupancy of family home: certain rights to occupy the family home, analogous to those for spouses and civil partners, can be

obtained by cohabitants under the Matrimonial Homes (Family Protection) (Scotland) Act 1981 and the Civil Partnership Act 2004. The right of occupancy is not, however, the same and there are three differences from the rights of spouses and civil partners. First, the right of cohabitants is not automatic and must be applied for in court. Secondly, the right if granted by the court is time limited to six months (though it may be extended on an unlimited number of occasions) rather than lasting, as with registered relationships, until the legal termination of the relationship. Thirdly, and perhaps most crucially, the right if granted is not good against third parties – in other words, the owner of the property can defeat his or her (ex-)partner's right granted by the court by the simple expedient of selling the property.

(2) Protection from domestic violence: the rules for interdicts and powers of arrest discussed above in relation to married couples and civil partners apply without substantive variation to cohabitants.

(3) Damages for wrongful death: just as a spouse or civil partner can seek damages on the negligently caused death of his or her partner under the Damages (Scotland) Act 2011, so too on the same terms and conditions can a cohabitant whose partner is negligently killed.

(4) Succession to tenancies: on the death of a tenant, his or her cohabitant is entitled to succeed to the tenancy, whether it is in the public sector (Housing (Scotland) Act 1988) or the private sector (Housing (Scotland) Act 2001).

(5) Joint adoption: cohabiting couples, so long as they are living together in an "enduring family relationship", are entitled to make a joint application to adopt a child under the Adoption and Children (Scotland) Act 2007. Non-conjugal couples (such as for example a mother and daughter) may not do so.

MAJOR LEGAL CONSEQUENCES OF COHABITATION: FINANCIAL READJUSTMENT AT END OF RELATIONSHIP

The two major legal consequences of cohabitation, applicable since the Family Law (Scotland) Act 2006 came into force, relate to the financial readjustment between the parties when the relationship comes to an end, either by death or by separation.

(1) Succession rights: under s 29 of the Family Law (Scotland) Act 2006, cohabitants have had limited succession rights in each other's estates. If a cohabitant dies intestate (that is to say, without a valid will) the survivor may ask the court to allocate some or all of the estate to him or her. This is not a claim of right, but a matter for the court's discretion, taking account of all the factors of the case, including other claims on the estate, any benefits (insurance, pensions and the like) that the survivor acquires as a result of his or her partner's death, and the size and nature of the estate. In no circumstances can the survivor be awarded more than he or she would have inherited had he or she been married to or in a civil partnership with the deceased. And if the deceased was, while cohabiting with the survivor, still in fact married or in a civil partnership with someone else, the surviving spouse or civil partner takes his or her prior rights and legal rights before the cohabitant's claim is determined.

(2) Financial claims on separation: also introduced by the Family Law (Scotland) Act 2006 are claims for financial readjustment between the parties when they separate before death (that is to say, they "split up"). These claims are much more limited than those available to spouses or civil partners, described in Chapter 10 below. A "s 28 claim" allows either ex-cohabitant to seek from the other a lump sum or such amount as may be specified, in one of two circumstances. First, a lump sum may be claimed to redress any imbalance in the financial and non-financial contributions of the cohabitants, economic advantages gained from and economic disadvantages suffered as a result of the cohabitation. If one cohabitant, in other words, has contributed more, suffered more or benefited more than the other (in either financial or other terms) then a lump sum can be claimed to restore the equilibrium between the parties. Secondly, such amount as may be specified by the court may be awarded in respect of the economic burden of caring, after the end of the cohabitation, for a child under 16 of whom the cohabitants are parents. So the parent with whom the child continues to reside can claim a share of his or her future costs from the other parent who is no longer living with them. As with a s 29 claim on death, a s 28 claim leaves much to the discretion of the court, but the underlying principle in s 28 is to achieve "fairness" between the parties.

Essential Facts

- A cohabiting couple is a couple who are "living together as husband and wife" or (if a same-sex couple) "living together as if married to each other".
- A cohabitant's claims for occupancy rights differ from those of a spouse or civil partner because they are not automatic, they last only six months if granted and they are not good against third parties.
- The court may make an award of a portion of a deceased's estate to the surviving cohabitant, but the claim is postponed to, and cannot be larger than, any claim of a surviving spouse or civil partner.
- The court may make an award of a capital sum from one ex-cohabitant to the other after separation if this is necessary to rebalance any contributions made or disadvantages suffered for the benefit of the relationship, or in order to share the future childcare costs.
- A claim under s 28 for sharing childcare costs can be made only in respect of a child of whom both cohabitants are the legal parents: it may not be made in respect of, say, a step-child.
- The assessment of the claim made by an ex-cohabitant on separation is based on fairness.

Essential Statutes

Matrimonial Homes (Family Protection) (Scotland) Act 1981

Section 18 extends to cohabiting couples (whether opposite-sex or same-sex) the provisions in the Act dealing with exclusion orders, and allows the court to grant occupancy rights similar to those arising automatically on marriage.

Family Law (Scotland) Act 2006

Section 25 defines cohabiting couples as a couple (whether opposite-sex or same-sex) who are or were living together as if they were married. Section 26 replicates for cohabiting couples the rule in the Family Law (Scotland) Act 1985 for spouses that there is a presumption that household goods are owned jointly in equal parts. Section 27 replicates for cohabiting couples the rule in the Family Law (Scotland) Act 1985 that savings from housekeeping money provided by one for the use of the other belongs to both equally.

Section 28 provides that when a cohabiting couple separates either may make a claim for financial provision against the other and the court may make an order requiring one to make a payment of a capital sum to the other, or an order requiring the payment of an amount in respect of the economic burden of caring for a child under 16 of whom both cohabitants are the parents. Section 29 allows a surviving cohabitant to ask the court to make an award to him or her out of the intestate estate of a deceased cohabitant on certain specified conditions.

Damages (Scotland) Act 2011

Section 4 provides that a person who negligently caused the death of a member of the pursuer's immediate family is liable to pay the survivor a sum to compensate for loss of support, distress and anxiety at the deceased's suffering, grief and sorrow at the relative's death and for loss of non-patrimonial benefit derived from the deceased's society. Section 14 defines "immediate family" to include cohabitants.

Essential Cases

Armour v Anderson (1994): Armour and Anderson lived together but Anderson was violent and Armour fled for her own safety. After some months she sought occupancy rights under the 1981 Act. Anderson's defence was that since Armour had fled she had terminated the cohabitation (which was a matter of fact) and therefore she was no longer a cohabitant and not entitled to seek cohabitants' occupancy rights.

The court rejected this defence and held that the time to determine whether a relationship of cohabitation exists is the time of the event that led to the court action, that is to say the event that led to Armour fleeing. Any other interpretation would mean that the Act's protective intent could never be given effect to.

Shilliday v Smith (1998): Isobel Shilliday and William Smith commenced living together and became engaged to be married. A house was purchased for them to live in but title was taken in the name of William alone. Nevertheless, Isobel paid for the renovations of the house. The marriage was called off and Isobel claimed back her money on the basis of unjustified enrichment.

The court held that the money should be repaid. The factor that made the enrichment "unjust" was that Isobel had paid the money in the expectation of getting married. When that expectation was frustrated it would be unjust to allow William to keep the benefit of the renovations to his house without cost.

Fitzpatrick v Sterling Housing Association (1999): John Thomson and Martin Fitzpatrick were a gay couple who had lived together for over twenty years in the house rented from a housing association by John. After a long illness John died and Martin sought to succeed to the tenancy. The Rent Act 1977 allowed the survivor of a couple who had "lived together as husband and wife" to succeed, as well as the survivor who was a member of the tenant's family. The landlord denied that John and Martin fulfilled either of these criteria: they could not be a "family" because they were gay.

The House of Lords held that a same-sex couple could not be said to "live together as husband and wife" but that they could be said to be "family". So Martin was able to remain living in his house (and the dam was burst for the full recognition of gay family rights in the UK).

Ghaidan v Mendoza (2004): this case differed from *Fitzpatrick* in that one of the gay couple died after the coming into force of the Human Rights Act 1998.

The House of Lords held that the phrase "living together as husband and wife" had now to be interpreted in a way that was not contrary to Arts 8 and 14 of the European Convention, which prohibited discrimination on the basis of sexual orientation. It was possible to read the phrase to include couples of the same sex who led their lives as married couples and so the survivor was able to succeed to the tenancy not only as a family member but also as a person who lived with the deceased "as husband or wife".

Gow v Grant 2012 UKSC 29: An older couple moved in together, with Gow selling her own flat and moving in to Grant's house. The couple then lived beyond their means for a few years, enjoying the good life. It didn't last, unfortunately, and the couple separated once the money ran out. Grant left the relationship with his house; Gow left the relationship with nothing. She sought an award under s 28 of the Family Law (Scotland) Act 2006, based on what the flat she had sold would have been worth had she kept it. The Inner House held that Gow was entitled to nothing since she could not establish that her selling of her flat was designed to give a benefit to Grant and in any case the point of s 28 was to correct a clear and quantifiable financial imbalance created by the relationship.

In the Supreme Court this decision was overruled, on the ground that the principle underlying s 28 was that of fairness: the court needed to look at the position of the individuals at the start of the relationship and compare it with their position at the end, and make such award as would be fair in the circumstances. Grant should therefore be ordered to pay an amount to Gow to compensate her for her loss.

Windram, Applicant 2009 Fam LR 157: Windram cohabited with her partner for twenty-four years and had two children with him. The partner died intestate and Windram made a claim under s 29 of the Family Law (Scotland) Act 2006, seeking a transfer of the family home and its furnishings into her name (it would go to the children otherwise).

The court held that it would be unfair to leave her with nothing and no security in her home; and that transfer of the house and furnishings would allow her to fulfil her responsibility to provide a home for her (and her partner's) children. So it made the order sought.

Kerr v Mangan 2014 CSIH 69: Mangan cohabited with Kerr for twenty-two years before his death: he died intestate. Most of his estate consisted in immoveable property situated in Ireland. Kerr made a claim under s 29 of the Family Law (Scotland) Act 2006, asking the court to award her a fair sum from Mangan's estate. Otherwise his property would go to his grown-up children. The question before the court was whether the property in Ireland should be included.

The normal private international law rule is that succession to immoveables is governed by the *lex situs*, that is to say the law of the place where the property is situated, but Kerr argued that a claim under s 29 was not a succession claim but a debt on the estate.

The Inner House held that the point of s 29 was to change the law of succession, allowing a claim when a person died which would have an effect on the succession. So the private international law rule applied, and the Irish property could not be affected by an order of the Scottish court made under s 29. Kerr received nothing, not because she deserved nothing but because there was no estate governed by s 29 from which to give her anything.

The more general importance of the case, however, is that the court pointed out that s 29 is very different from s 28. That section, the Supreme Court had explained, was based on fairness, but s 29 had no such underpinning. Indeed, the Court of Session struggled to find any rational principle upon which a court could assess how much to give under s 29.

8 DEREGISTERING RELATIONSHIPS BY DIVORCE OR DISSOLUTION

Marriage and civil partnership are matters of legal status while cohabitation is a mere matter of fact: status is acquired on registration of the relationship. It follows that to escape from the legal consequences of cohabitation one simply needs to change the facts (that is to say, stop cohabiting), but to escape from the legal consequences of marriage or civil partnership one must go through a legal process to remove the legal status, to "deregister", if you like. For marriage the process of deregistration is called divorce and for civil partnership the process is called dissolution. The grounds are substantially, but not exactly, the same.

In modern Scots law there are only two grounds for divorce or dissolution: the obtaining of an interim gender recognition certificate by one of the partners (that is to say, that individual's taking steps to have his or her sex-change formally recognised), or the irretrievable breakdown of the relationship (Divorce (Scotland) Act 1976, s 1(1); Civil Partnership Act 2004, s 117). The statutes go on to state when, but only when, irretrievable breakdown has occurred and if the facts specified exist then the marriage or civil partnership has broken down in the eyes of the law (irrespective of whether the actual relationship has broken down or not), and if the facts specified do not exist then the marriage or civil partnership has not broken down in the eyes of the law (irrespective of whether the actual relationship survives or not). There are four sets of facts that will deem a marriage to have broken down irretrievably (or, to put it more realistically, there are four sets of facts that justify a divorce); and there are three sets of facts that will deem a civil partnership to have broken down irretrievably and will justify a dissolution.

ADULTERY

Adultery is (heterosexual) sexual intercourse by a married person with another person not his or her spouse; it is, like all the grounds for divorce, available whether the marriage is between a same-sex couple or an opposite-sex couple. But adultery is the only ground for divorce that does not also give a ground to dissolve a civil partnership. It is organ-specific and it requires the insertion of a penis into a vagina. Any other sexual act is not adultery and so same-sex sexual activity or any opposite-sex sexual activity other than full penile penetration of the vagina is not in itself absolute proof that the marriage has broken down irretrievably. The adultery must have occurred since the date of the marriage, and one occurrence is sufficient to destroy the marriage. There are a number of defences to an action for divorce based on adultery. First, it is a defence if the pursuer has connived in the act (Divorce (Scotland) Act 1976, s 1(3) which gives statutory effect to the common law defence known as *lenocinium*). This is to prevent parties from seeking an immediate divorce from each other by deciding together that one will provide a ground for the other to use: parties who agree to divorce ought not (in the eyes of the law) to be allowed to do so immediately and they are forced to wait a year – see below). Secondly, if the pursuer has condoned the act of adultery by the defender then he or she cannot use that act as a ground for divorce. Condonation at common law was forgiveness and though the word "condonation" continues to be used by the statute, actual forgiveness is no longer the issue. Rather, "condonation" is proved by the pursuer cohabiting or continuing to cohabit with the defender three months after cohabiting at any point after discovering the fact of the adultery (Divorce (Scotland) Act 1976, s 2(2) and (4)). Though the wording of the statute is obscure, the rule is not that condonation is created by three months of continuous cohabitation. The length of cohabitation is irrelevant, so long as there is cohabitation at two points in time: one after the discovery of the adultery, and the second at any point at least three months after that initial period of cohabitation. Condonation, like *lenocinium*, bars the divorce on this ground.

UNREASONABLE BEHAVIOUR

This ground applies to both marriage and civil partnership, though in truth it is not the behaviour that needs to be unreasonable. The actual ground is that the defender has acted in such a way that the pursuer cannot reasonably be expected to continue to cohabit with the defender. So it is the expectation of continued cohabitation rather than the behaviour itself that needs to be shown to be unreasonable. The behaviour that would justify a divorce or dissolution may be something that the defender cannot be blamed for, for example behaviour as a result of a mental illness. And it may be either active or passive, though the difference between passive behaviour and non-behaviour is sometimes not very clear. For example, there would seem to be little doubt that refusing to speak to one's spouse or civil partner would be passive behaviour; but it might be that failing ever to give birthday, anniversary or other special occasion presents is non-behaviour and so not relevant for this ground of divorce or dissolution. Examples of active behaviour would include, but is not limited to, physical violence towards the other, non-physical behaviour such as verbal abuse, habitual drunkenness even when not resulting in violence, persistent lying, excessive demands for sex, refusal of any sex or knowingly making false accusations against the other.

NON-COHABITATION WITH CONSENT

If the defender consents to the divorce or dissolution then the marriage or civil partnership has irretrievably broken down once a year has passed during which the parties did not live together as a married couple or as civil partners. It frequently happens that within volatile relationships, or after an initial separation, the parties get back together again to see whether they can patch up their differences and recommence their conjugal life together. It would be bad social policy if the law did anything to discourage this, such as by threatening to have the period of a year start running again if the reconciliation attempt fails. So the Divorce (Scotland) Act 1976 and the Civil Partnership Act 2004 allow parties to live together as a married couple or as civil partners for a period or periods of up to six months without interrupting the running of the one-year period. Of course the time that the couple spend together does not count towards the one year, but it does not stop it and require the whole period to be recommenced. So, for example, if a couple separate on 1 January, attempt reconciliation by moving back together on 1 August, but permanently separate on 1 September, the ground of divorce or dissolution based on one year's non-cohabitation with consent to the termination of the relationship is acquired one year and one month after the initial separation, that is to say in our example thirteen months after 1 January.

NON-COHABITATION WITHOUT CONSENT

If the defender refuses to agree to the divorce or dissolution, and no other ground for termination exists, the pursuer must wait until there have been two years in which the parties did not live together as a married couple or as civil partners. As with the one-year period, the parties are entitled, without losing this ground for divorce or dissolution, to live together for up to six months, which period or periods will not count towards the two years.

Essential Facts

- Adultery and unreasonable behaviour justify an immediate divorce; the latter (but not the former) also justifies the immediate dissolution of a civil partnership.
- Connivance at, or condonation of, the other's adultery deprives a pursuer of this ground for divorce.
- It is, in reality, not the behaviour that needs to be unreasonable but the continued expectation that the other spouse or civil partner should continue to live with someone who behaves that way.
- Non-cohabitation for one year with the consent of the other or non-cohabitation for two years without consent are the two no-fault grounds of divorce and dissolution in Scots law.
- The granting of an interim gender recognition certificate to a person currently married or in a civil partnership gives a ground of divorce or dissolution to both parties. This will become a full gender recognition certificate once the divorce or dissolution has been granted.

Essential Statutes

Divorce (Scotland) Act 1976

Section 1(1) provides that the only two grounds for divorce in Scots law are (i) irretrievable breakdown of marriage and (ii) the obtaining of an interim gender recognition certificate. Section 1(2) sets out the only circumstances in which irretrievable breakdown of marriage can be established: (a) adultery; (b) unreasonable behaviour; (d), non-cohabitation between the parties for one year and the defender's consent to the divorce; (e) two years non-cohabitation between the parties. Section 2 provides that adultery is not condoned unless there has been cohabitation between the parties at certain stated periods, and that no account is to be taken of cohabitation for up to six months in counting the non-cohabitation periods.

Civil Partnership Act 2004

Sections 117 to 119 replicate for civil partners the provisions in ss 1 and 2 of the Divorce (Scotland) Act 1976, except that adultery (as in s 1(2)(a) of the 1976 Act) is not made a ground in s 177 of the 2004 Act for the dissolution of a civil partnership.

Marriage and Civil Partnership (Scotland) Act 2014

Section 5(2) amends s 1 of the 1976 Act to ensure that adultery has the same meaning within the context of same-sex marriages as it has within the context of opposite-sex marriages.

Essential Cases

Hunter v Hunter (1900): Mrs Hunter's husband had deserted her and run off to Canada and had not contacted her for a period of time. So she assumed he was dead and contracted a new "marriage" with her cousin. When the husband reappeared, he sought a divorce on the basis of her adultery. Mrs Hunter's defence was that she had no *mens rea* for this matrimonial offence since she believed her husband was dead. The court, however, formed the opinion that she had been lax in not obtaining a divorce which she had been legally entitled to as her husband had deserted her. She was therefore held to be guilty of adultery and the divorce was granted.

Thomson v Thomson (1908): a wife asked her husband for money to go on an innocent day trip; in fact, she was planning to meet her lover. Her duplicitous husband knew this (though she did not know that he knew) and he gave her the money in the hope that she would meet the lover, commit adultery and so give him a ground for divorce. The wife took the money and committed adultery; when her husband sued her for divorce, she pleaded *lenocinium*: she claimed that by knowingly giving her the wherewithal to meet the lover Mr Thomson was actively encouraging her to commit adultery.

The court rejected this defence on the basis that the wife did not understand herself to be acting upon the husband's encouragement (that is to say there was no collusion since the wife was deceived as to the husband's motives).

MacLennan v MacLennan (1958): Mrs MacLennan left her husband and went to the USA for some months. When she returned to Scotland she was found to be pregnant and her husband sued her for divorce for adultery. Her defence was that she had become pregnant through artificial insemination and so could not be sued for adultery, which required sexual intercourse.

The court agreed that artificial insemination did not amount to adultery (though in fact the divorce was granted since she did not prove her story). The case is memorable for Lord Wheatley's graphic description of adultery as being "physical contact with an alien and unlawful sexual organ".

Lennie v Lennie (1950): Mr and Mrs Lennie lived together but Mrs Lennie refused to permit sexual relations. Mr Lennie sued her for divorce on the basis that this amounted to desertion (withdrawal from living together as husband and wife) which until 2006 was another ground of divorce.

The court held that there was more to living together as husband and wife than sexual relations and that the termination (even by one party against the wishes of the other) of sexual relations was not in itself sufficient to amount to desertion. Nor, today, would it amount to non–cohabitation. Whether it would amount to unreasonable behaviour would depend upon whether the court held that in the circumstances it was unreasonable to expect the one who wanted the sex to continue to live with the one who was withholding it. The case remains authority for the proposition that a couple can live together as a married couple even although there is no sexual activity between the two.

Hastie v Hastie (1985): Mr and Mrs Hastie separated and were involved in a bitter custody dispute over who would get their daughter. In the course of that dispute Mrs Hastie made an allegation that her husband had committed incest with their daughter. She later admitted that this mendacity had been invented in order to ruin her opponent's chances in the custody dispute.

The court held that though a single event, this deliberately false allegation was so destructive of the marital relationship that it amounted to behaviour such that it was unreasonable to expect the pursuer to continue living with the defender. Mr Hastie was granted a divorce on that basis.

Findlay v Findlay (1991): Mr Findlay kept late hours and Mrs Findlay did not like it. This was not, in itself, sufficient to amount to behaviour such that it was unreasonable to expect Mrs Findlay to continue living with her husband and so she did not have any ground to divorce him. But she left him, nevertheless. She subsequently formed an association with another man and at this stage sued her husband for unreasonable behaviour.

The court held that it was unreasonable to expect Mrs Findlay, happy with her new man, to return to Mr Findlay with whom she was unhappy and therefore the ground of divorce was now made out.

9 DEREGISTERING RELATIONSHIPS BY ANNULMENT

If a party to a marriage or civil partnership wishes to escape from their legal relationship but does not for some reason wish to seek a divorce or dissolution, an alternative is to seek to have the marriage or civil partnership annulled instead. In other words, a party may attempt to persuade the court that the marriage or civil partnership was never valid in the first place. It is not possible to found upon minor irregularities in the process of entering into the marriage or civil partnership, such as that the celebrant was not properly authorised, or the place of marriage or civil partnership was not as stated in the marriage notice and marriage schedule. Section 23A of the Marriage (Scotland) Act 1977 and s 95A of the Civil Partnership Act 2004 provides that irregularities of this nature will be ignored. This is because a marriage or civil partnership is not a contract but is a status and there are strong public policy reasons to uphold marriage and civil partnership against challenges on matters of little social import. However, a marriage or civil partnership can be annulled, that is to say declared never to have been valid, if the irregularity affects an issue that goes to the essence of the status of marriage or civil partnership, such as for example the capacity of the party to enter into it. There are numerous grounds available to a party who wishes to challenge the validity of a marriage or civil partnership.

AGE

If the parties are not old enough to marry or register a civil partnership, any purported marriage or civil partnership is null and void *ab initio* (that is to say, from the very start). A marriage ceremony or civil partnership registration which takes place in Scotland will create a valid marriage or civil partnership only if both parties are over the age of 16 (Marriage (Scotland) Act 1977, s 1(2); Civil Partnership Act 2004, s 86(1)(c)), and it does not matter for the application of this rule that one of the parties comes from a country where the age of marriage or civil partnership is lower. And the age of 16 is the age of marriage and civil partnership for all persons domiciled in Scotland no matter where in the world the marriage or civil partnership takes place (Marriage (Scotland) Act 1977, s 1(1); Civil Partnership Act 2004, s 217(4)). It follows that if the marriage took place or the civil partnership was registered in Scotland at any time before either party's 16th birthday, or it took place abroad before the Scottish party's 16th birthday, the marriage or civil partnership is fatally flawed and has no legal effect. A civil partnership involving a Scottish person over the age of 16 cannot take place if the other party is under 16, even in a country with a lower age limit than Scotland (none at the moment, it is fair to point out, does). The rule is different with marriage (even involving a same-sex couple) and a 16 year old may marry abroad a foreign 15 year old if the 15 year old's legal system allows this.

Sometimes the age of marriage is 21 in Scotland. A person who wishes to marry or enter a civil partnership with an affinitive relative (defined below) in circumstances in which the law allows this may do so only after they are both 21 years of age or older (Marriage (Scotland) Act 1977, s 2; Civil Partnership Act 2004, s 86(3)).

THE FORBIDDEN DEGREES

If the parties to the marriage or civil partnership are within the forbidden degrees of relationship they are incapable of marrying each other or registering a civil partnership with each other (Marriage (Scotland) Act 1977, s 2; Civil Partnership Act 2004, Sch 10), and any purported marriage or civil partnership between parties within these relationships is null and void. There are three categories of forbidden degree: consanguine, adoptive and affinitive.

Consanguine relationships are relationships of blood. A person may not marry or enter into a civil partnership with his or her parent, grandparent, great-grandparent, child, grandchild, great-grandchild, sibling, aunt, uncle, niece or nephew. Adoptive relationships are created through an adoption order made by a court of competent jurisdiction. A person may not marry or enter into a civil partnership with his or her adoptive parent or adopted child (though he or she may do so with any other relative traced through the adoptive parent or child). Affinitive relationships are created through marriage or civil partnership and, unless the exception applies, a person may not marry or enter into a civil partnership with the ex-spouse or ex-civil partner of his or her parent. The exception, permitting marriage or civil partnership within step-relationships, is if the parties never lived in family with each other before the younger reached the age of 18, the older never treated the younger as a child of the family and they are both now over the age of 21.

WRONG GENDER MIX

Between 2004, when civil partnership was introduced, and 2014, when marriage was opened to same-sex couples, the law of Scotland treated marriage and civil partnership as fundamentally different institutions, notwithstanding the fact that the legal consequences of each, capacities to enter and rules for exit were (and are) substantially the same. The crucial difference between the two institutions was that marriage was limited in its availability to opposite-sex couples while civil partnership was limited in its availability to same-sex couples. This changed with the Marriage and Civil Partnership (Scotland) Act 2014, which opened marriage to same-sex couples, rendering marriage gender-neutral (at least from the point of view of the parties – registration of celebrants still draws a distinction between opposite-sex and same-sex marriage). Oddly, the 2014 Act retained civil partnership as an exclusively same-sex (that is to say non-gender-neutral) institution, with the result that a civil partnership is void if entered into by an opposite-sex couple (Civil Partnership Act 2004, s 86(1)(a)). It is entirely unclear whether this rule is limited to civil partnerships registered in the United Kingdom, or whether it would also prevent the recognition of an opposite-sex civil partnership validly entered into in a foreign country that allows this (such as New Zealand or South Africa).

People who have undergone gender realignment surgery and who live their lives in the opposite gender to that which appears on their birth certificates remain in law the original gender for the purposes of marriage and civil partnership, until they acquire a gender recognition certificate granted under the terms of the Gender Recognition Act 2004. Once that certificate has been obtained they can enter a civil partnership in their acquired gender. If a spouse or civil partner changes gender while still married or in a civil partnership then he or she can acquire only an interim gender recognition certificate (which gives a ground to terminate the marriage or civil partnership by divorce) unless the couple wish the relationship to continue, in which case a full gender recognition certificate will be issued and the civil partnership will automatically become a marriage (or the pre-existing marriage will become a marriage with a different gender mix).

EXISTING MARRIAGE OR CIVIL PARTNERSHIP

Marriage has always been in Scotland, and civil partnership is statutorily, a monogamous relationship and it follows that an individual who is already a party to one or other of these institutions may not enter into another one without the first ending (either through death of the partner, or divorce, dissolution or annulment). If they purport to do so, the subsequent marriage or civil partnership is null and void. This is not to say that polygamous marriages validly entered into in another legal system which allows this will not be recognised here as a marriage. Rather, so long as the parties had capacity to enter into a multiple-person relationship and they did so in a country that treats multiple-person relationships as marriage, the parties thereto will be regarded as married in this country for most purposes (Matrimonial Proceedings (Polygamous Marriages) Act 1972, as amended by Private International Law (Miscellaneous Provisions) Act 1995). No jurisdiction that permits civil partnership has allowed it to be entered into polygamously and so the issue would not arise with civil partners.

LACK OF CAPACITY TO UNDERSTAND

The above grounds upon which a marriage or civil partnership can be annulled are relatively straightforward to deal with since the facts at issue are usually very easy to establish. Proof of age or gender or existing relationship is seldom susceptible to doubt or uncertainty. Incapacity to understand, however, is very different for there is much room for uncertainty and different interpretation of the facts that can be proved.

The basic rule is that a person who was at the time of the marriage ceremony or civil partnership registration incapable of understanding the nature of marriage or civil partnership and of consenting thereto is not able for that reason to enter a marriage or civil partnership. Any purported consent is of no effect and the marriage or civil partnership based on such purported consent is null and void. However, it has always been the view of the law that marriage (and the same, presumably, can be said of civil partnership) is a simple concept, easy to understand and understood by most people even if of very low intelligence. It follows that to escape a marriage or civil partnership on an assertion that one of the parties did not understand its nature, the claimant must show that the party's ability to understand anything is very severely compromised. A person who does not have the intellectual capacity to make a will or enter into a contract may well be at the same time able to understand the simple institution of marriage. There is no room for the argument that a person's consent to marriage or civil partnership is void as having been obtained through facility and circumvention (that is to say, simple-mindedness and undue pressure). The onus on the person seeking to have the marriage or civil partnership annulled on this ground is heavy.

COMPROMISED CONSENT

It is sometimes argued that a person's consent to marriage or civil partnership, though apparently valid and given by a person with full capacity to consent, has been obtained by fraud, or that the person whose consent is at issue is under a vitiating error of understanding: in these circumstances the court may annul the marriage or civil partnership. But it will be slow to do so and there is no possibility of a marriage or civil partnership being annulled on the basis of error as to the quality of the partner one is acquiring. A woman who marries a man believing him to be rich and good, does not have an invalid marriage just because she discovers that he has been lying to her and he is destitute and cruel. A man who marries a woman because he believes that the child she is carrying is his cannot have that marriage annulled on the basis of mistake if he were to discover that the child was in fact fathered by another man. Error is relevant only when it goes to the very identity of the other party or of the nature of the ceremony (Marriage (Scotland) Act 1977, s 20A(5); Civil Partnership Act 2004, s 123(2); both as amended by the Family Law (Scotland) Act 2006). Given that the presence of both at the ceremony of marriage or civil partnership registration is required, error as to identity, while conceivable, is highly unlikely ever to occur in Scotland.

Consent, to be valid, is consent to be married or consent to have a civil partnership registered. Consent to anything else does not make marriage or civil partnership. Occasionally the Scottish court held that if one of the parties, while appearing to consent to marriage, is not in fact agreeing to enter into the lawful status of marriage with the other person but is consenting only to the obtaining of some extraneous benefit (for example immigration) then the marriage can be declared null for lack of consent. This was a dangerous doctrine, but "tacitly withholding consent" was abolished as a ground upon which a marriage or civil partnership could be annulled by the Family Law (Scotland) Act 2006, s 2 and Sch 1.

However, if a person is forced into marriage against his or her will, and has given consent only through fear of bodily or mental injury, then that consent is not genuine and the marriage or civil partnership may be annulled for lack of consent. There is here an important (though some-times subtle) difference between an arranged marriage (which is legitimate) and a forced marriage (which is not). The issue is unlikely to arise in the context of civil partnership or same-sex marriage. The Forced Marriage etc (Protection and Jurisdiction) (Scotland) Act 2011 provides for court orders to protect people at risk of being forced into marriage against their wills. If a person subject to such a risk is a child, or a child lives with such a person, the child can be referred to a children's hearing (discussed in Chapter 5 above) which might impose a protective compulsory supervision order on the child.

IMPOTENCY

There is one ground for having a marriage annulled that does not apply to either civil partnerships or marriages involving same-sex couples. And this ground is unique even within opposite-sex marriage in that it presupposes a valid marriage at the time it was entered into, but which can be retrospectively annulled if one or other of the parties seeks to escape it: unless and until this happens, the marriage is valid (unlike any of the other grounds whereby the marriage or civil partnership is held to be void from the beginning, or void *ab initio*). The marriage is therefore not void but merely voidable. In reality this is divorce by pretending the marriage never was, and is important for those who do not believe in, but want to benefit from, divorce. The ground is the incurable impotency of one or other of the parties at the time of the marriage.

Impotency, like adultery, is organ-specific and is the inability (whether caused by mental inhibition or physical incapacity) to achieve full penile penetration of the vagina. Ability or inability to indulge in any other sort of sexual activity is not relevant (which explains its inapplicability to same-sex marriage). Ability or inability to achieve full sexual intercourse with another person is not relevant. Ability or inability to have children is not relevant. Impotency is no more nor any less than the inability to achieve full penile penetration of the vagina with one's marriage partner. Impotency, to be relevant, must exist at the date of the marriage, and it must be at that point in time incurable (though scientific developments providing a cure subsequently are also irrelevant).

No same-sex relationship, whether civil partnership or marriage, requires the ability of one partner to penetrate in a sexual manner any part of the other's body before the relationship is complete and unchallengeable – same-sex couples are free from the anomalous concept of a voidable relationship because they are (at least vis-à-vis each other) never impotent.

Essential Facts

- Marriage and civil partnership can only be entered into in Scotland if both parties are over the age of 16 years; Scottish domiciliaries may not marry nor enter into a civil partnership anywhere in the world before their 16th birthday.
- The forbidden degrees of marriage and civil partnership are: (i) parent, child, grandparent, grandchild, great-grandparent, great-grandchild, brother, sister, uncle, aunt, nephew and niece; (ii) adoptive or former adoptive parent, adopted or former adopted child; (iii) step-parent, stepchild. There are some exceptions to (iii) but none to (i) or (ii).
- Marriage and civil partnership may only be entered into in the UK monogamously; UK law sometimes, however, recognises foreign polygamous marriages.
- You take your partner for better or for worse, so your consent is not vitiated by any error you make about the quality of your partner, except his or her identity.
- Consent to marriage or civil partnership may be vitiated if it has been obtained by duress, with threats to physical or mental wellbeing.
- An opposite-sex marriage (but not a same-sex marriage or a civil partnership) is voidable (that is to say is valid until challenged) if one of the parties was incurably impotent at the time of the marriage.

Essential Statutes

Matrimonial Proceedings (Polygamous Marriages) Act 1972

Section 2 allows the Scottish court to hear actions for divorce to bring to an end marriages that are actually or potentially polygamous.

Marriage (Scotland) Act 1977

Section 1 sets down the age of 16 for all marriages that take place in Scotland, and for all persons domiciled in Scotland wherever in the world they marry. Section 2 and Schedule 1 set out the forbidden degrees of marriage. Section 20A(1)–(3) provides that a marriage is void if the party consenting to it was (i) capable to consenting but did so by reason only of duress or error or (ii) incapable of understanding the nature of marriage and consenting to it. Section 20A(5) provides that "error" in this context means only error as to the nature of the ceremony or the identity of the other party. Section 20A(4) provides that a marriage is not void only because the party tacitly withheld consent. Section 23A provides that a marriage where both parties were present at the ceremony and which has been registered cannot be challenged on the ground of failure to comply with any of the formalities laid down in the 1977 Act, though it may still be challenged if it has breached the rules relating to age of the parties or the forbidden degrees.

Private International Law (Miscellaneous Provisions) Act 1995

Section 7 permits a person domiciled in Scotland to marry abroad under a system that permits polygamy, so long as the marriage itself is not polygamous.

Civil Partnership Act 2004

Section 86(1)–(5) and Schedule 10 replicate for civil partnership the rules of age and forbidden degrees found in ss 1 and 2 of and Schedule to the Marriage (Scotland) Act 1977.

Section 95A replicates for civil partnership the rule in s 23A of the Marriage (Scotland) Act 1977 saving marriages with flawed formalities.

Forced Marriage etc (Protection and Jurisdiction) (Scotland) Act 2011

Section 1 allows the court to make an order protecting a person from being forced into a marriage. Section 9 makes it an offence to breach an order under the statute.

Marriage and Civil Partnership (Scotland) Act 2014

Section 5(1) provides that the rule allowing a marriage to be annulled on the ground of impotency applies only to opposite-sex marriages.

Essential Cases

F v F (1945): Mr F raised an action against his wife, seeking to have their marriage declared a nullity on the ground of his own incurable impotency at the date of the wedding. In the past actions had only been raised by the potent partner against the impotent partner. But the court held that it was only third parties who were excluded from raising actions based on impotency and so there was nothing to prevent Mr F seeking nullity of marriage on the basis of his own impotency.

Lang v Lang (1921): Walter Lang, a seaman from Leith, was invited by Violette Pieroni, spinster of that parish, to spend the night with her. He did so, and repeated the experience on numerous occasions. When informed by Violette that she was pregnant, he married her. In fact, Violette had been having sex with someone else before Seaman Lang came along and the child was not her husband's. He sought a declarator of invalidity of marriage on the ground that his consent was based on a false premise, that the child was his.

The court held that consent given in error as to the quality of the other party is irrelevant: only error as to the identity of the other will render the consent invalid. Declarator of nullity was refused.

Corbett v Corbett (1971): George Jamieson became April Ashley and married Arthur Corbett. When that relationship collapsed, April sued for divorce and Arthur pleaded the marriage was null and void as having been between two men.

The court held that April was not "female" for the purposes of marriage since she could not perform "the essential role of a woman" in marriage, which was to provide a natural and not an artificial vagina for the satisfaction of her husband.

Bellinger v Bellinger (2003): Mr and Mrs Bellinger had been married for twenty years, Mr Bellinger having entered into the marriage fully aware that Mrs Bellinger had been born male and had undergone gender reassignment surgery. They sought a declaration that their marriage was valid.

The House of Lords accepted that *Corbett* continued to represent English law and that biological factors determined gender for the purposes of marriage. It followed that Mr and Mrs Bellinger were both men and the marriage was void. They issued, however, a declaration of incompatibility with the European Convention on Human Rights (ECHR) since the European Court had earlier held the *Corbett* rule to be contrary to both Arts 8 and 12 (*Goodwin* v *United Kingdom* (2002)). The Gender Recognition Act 2004 reversed the result of this case (and, of course, of *Corbett*).

Mahmud v Mahmud (1994): Shahid Mahmud lived with his girlfriend Lesley Scott and their child. His parents arranged for him to marry his cousin, whom they imported from Pakistan for the purpose. Though initially he refused, he eventually gave in to the family pressure put upon him (he was threatened that shame and degradation would be visited upon the whole family unless he submitted to the marriage arranged by his parents). Immediately after the marriage ceremony, he returned home to Lesley and their child. The wife was soon thereafter deported back from whence she came (where she led a humiliated life, unmarriable but without a husband). Shahid now sought a declarator of nullity on the basis that his consent had been forced from him through the duress of his family.

Lord Prosser held that his will had been overborne and his consent was vitiated, with the result that the marriage was null and void.

Singh v Singh (2005): June Kaur was 18 years old, with a boyfriend called Keith Singh, when her mother took her to India and married her off, against her will, to a man she did not know, called Bikramjit Singh. June was taken to her new husband's house but she refused to have sex with him and a week later she returned home to Scotland. She moved out of her parents' house and went to live with Keith. She now sought a declarator that she had not given valid consent to her marriage which was, therefore, void.

The court found that June's mother had threatened to destroy her passport, leaving her stranded in India, if she did not submit. It held that this threat of immediate danger to June's liberty, causing her will to be overborne, vitiated her consent. But the judge also sounded a cautionary note. The threats had to be of immediate danger to life, limb or liberty. He doubted whether the threats in the earlier case of *Mahmud* v *Mahmud* (above) satisfied this test.

A v K (2011): the pursuer was a UK citizen of Pakistani ethnicity. When she was 20 years old, during a period of depression, she met a man on the internet. He was Pakistani, living in that country but wanting to move to the UK. He proposed marriage. She accepted, and they were married, over the telephone, while she was in Scotland and he was in Pakistan. Also involved, apparently as a celebrant, seemed to be a man (in Pakistan) who claimed to be a priest. Such a marriage would be valid in Pakistan but invalid in Scotland where it is an absolute rule for all marriages taking place in Scotland that the parties and the celebrant must be physically present in front of each other. But where did this marriage take place?

The formal validity of a marriage is determined by the law of the place where the formalities occurred. The judge held that this marriage took place in Pakistan, where both the husband and the celebrant were located, and so the marriage was valid. If the wife wanted out of it, her remedy was to seek a divorce (or annulment) from the courts in Pakistan.

10 FINANCIAL PROVISION ON DIVORCE, DISSOLUTION AND ANNULMENT

Whenever a court brings a marriage or civil partnership to an end, whether by divorce, dissolution or annulment, it is empowered to make orders for financial readjustment between the parties. In other words, the court is entitled to order one ex-partner to transfer some of his or her property or make a cash payment to the other ex-partner, and even to make a periodical payment thereto. Prior to the Family Law (Scotland) Act 1985 the court's power to do so at the end of a marriage was virtually unlimited but exercised extremely narrowly: the spousal obligation of aliment was continued on divorce by requiring the wealthier ex-spouse (nearly always the ex-husband) to make a periodical allowance to the other, which was to last for the rest of the life of the other (or until her remarriage and acquisition thereby of another source of support).

There were, however, a number of unfortunate consequences to this. First, it maintained a relationship between the parties after the end of their marriage though that relationship was reduced to one of pure financial giving and taking. Second, it encouraged the receiver to expect to continue to receive and did nothing to encourage her (and it usually was a woman) to attempt to regain a position of independence. Third, it emphasised female dependency on male earning power. The 1985 Act attempted to change all that by introducing into the law the philosophy of the "clean break". Now, on divorce, dissolution or annulment, the court is encouraged to deal with the parties' joint finances in a "once and for all" manner, in order to even out the financial inequities that are inevitable in many relationships and to put both parties on the road to financial independence, rather than to ensure that one continues to be able to rely on the other for life. A periodical allowance may still be made, but only when it is proved that a clean break settlement is inappropriate in the special circumstances of the case or is inadequate.

The court has the power to make a range of orders, including an order requiring a property owner to transfer items of property to his or her ex-partner, requiring one party to make a financial payment to the other, an order splitting the pension fund of one so that the other has a pension too, requiring the payment on a regular basis of a periodical allowance to the other and various incidental orders such as valuation and sale of property (Family Law (Scotland) Act 1985, s 8(1)). Before any order can be made by the court two separate tests must be satisfied. First, the order must be reasonable having regard to the resources of the parties. So it will seldom be appropriate to order one ex-partner to pay over all he or she has to the other, or to require him or her to make a periodical allowance greater than his or her own income. Secondly, and far more problematically, the order must be justified by one of the principles laid down in s 9(1) of the 1985 Act (the "s 9 Principles"). In other words, in order to make a claim for financial provision on divorce, dissolution or annulment, the claimant must justify that claim by reference to one or more of the s 9 Principles. A claim will not be relevant if justified on any other basis. But even where a claim can be justified by one or more of the s 9 Principles, the court retains the final discretion and may not, in the circumstances of the case, make any order at all.

However, notwithstanding its discretion, 30 years of application of the Act has shown that the Scottish courts will treat the application of the first principle (fair sharing of matrimonial property) as virtually a claim of right which every divorcing or dissolving couple should expect to receive or to pay; the other principles may be applied in the particular circumstances of the case, or it may be regarded that the payment made under the first principle also satisfies any claim that can be justified by any of the other principles.

FAIR SHARING OF MATRIMONIAL PROPERTY: GENERAL

The first of the s 9 Principles is contained in s 9(1)(a) of the 1985 Act and it is that "the net value of the matrimonial property should be shared fairly between the parties to the marriage". This apparently simple statement is full of legal complexities, which students must grasp since this Principle is far and away the most important of them all. There are four concepts contained within the Principle that need discussing.

FAIR SHARING OF MATRIMONIAL PROPERTY: "NET VALUE"

Net value is the value of the property subject to deduction of debts due upon the property. The easiest case is that of the family home that is subject to a mortgage. If, for example, the parties live in a house valued at £250,000 but there is a mortgage of £200,000 on the property then the net value, available for sharing under this principle, is £50,000. While that is straightforward, what has proved difficult for the court is the process of valuation. There is often a difference between the price one party's valuers put on an item of property and the price the other party's valuers put on it, for valuation is seldom an exact science. As a general rule it is for the claimant to establish to the court the accuracy of the valuation he or she claims a share of. Value is sometimes affected by whose eyes it is seen from. The market value of a house or a business may not be the "value" that a seller receives for it, if, for example, there is a charge to capital gains tax when it is sold, or some other penalty is imposed on its sale (such as, for example, repaying the discount received when an ex-council house tenant has bought his or her home and subsequently sells it). The Court of Session resolved many years of doubt in 2003 by holding that "value" for the purpose of the 1985 Act is market value and not the net profit gained by the person who disposes of the property.

FAIR SHARING OF MATRIMONIAL PROPERTY: THE RELEVANT DATE

Another difficulty with "net value" is the date upon which it is valued. The statute makes plain that the property that is to be shared fairly under this principle is the net value, assessed at the "relevant date". This is, basically, the date the parties finally separated (though the precise date can sometimes be disputed if parties gradually drift apart). And since the relevant date can often be some years prior to the actual action for divorce it may be that the property substantially increases or decreases in value. In that situation it is still the value at the date of separation that is to be shared, for that is all that is justified by s 9(1)(a). So if civil partners separate in 2010 and there is a house with a net worth of £110,000 at that time, but when they seek dissolution of their civil partnership in 2015 the house has a net worth of £160,000, s 9(1)(a) justifies only the fair sharing of £110,000. If the financial provision that the court decides to make is to order a transfer of property that has increased in its value, then sometimes the value at the date of transfer rather than the relevant date will be used for that purpose (Family Law (Scotland) Act 2006, s 16, amending the 1985 Act). But the "relevant date" rule can work both ways. If a man owns shares worth £50,000 at the relevant date but on the date of divorce or dissolution they are now worth £20,000, his ex-wife or ex-husband or ex-civil partner would in principle be entitled under s 9(1)(a) to receive shares worth half of £50,000, even though that is no longer half of what the man now owns. The potential unfairness of that is ameliorated by the power of the court to take account of available resources.

FAIR SHARING OF MATRIMONIAL PROPERTY: MEANING OF "MATRIMONIAL PROPERTY"

The most difficult part of this principle is the concept of matrimonial property itself (called "partnership property" for the purposes of civil partnership). The key to understanding s 9(1)(a) is to recognise that the principle contained therein justifies a fair sharing of only that property that comes within the highly technical definition of "matrimonial property": this is *not* all the property the parties own, either jointly or singly, but only that property coming within the definition contained in s 10 (4) of the 1985 Act. The parties are very likely to own other property than "matrimonial property" but if an ex-spouse wants a share of that other property on divorce, dissolution or annulment, he or she must justify that claim by a Principle other than that contained in s 9(1)(a).

Section 10(4) defines "matrimonial property" as all the property belonging to the parties or either of them at the relevant date which was acquired by them or him or her (otherwise than by way of gift or succession from a third party) during the marriage or civil partnership but before the relevant date. The moment of acquisition is crucial here. Property becomes "matrimonial property" (and therefore available for fair sharing under s 9(1)(a)) if it was acquired by either party at some point in time between the moment the legal relationship is established (the date of the marriage or of the registration of the civil partnership) and the relevant date. So, property owned by the parties before the marriage or civil partnership is not (subject to the exception mentioned immediately below) "matrimonial property"; property acquired after the relevant date is not "matrimonial property"; property acquired by way of gift or succession from a third party is not "matrimonial property". The exception to the date of acquisition is that property may be "matrimonial property" for this purpose if it was acquired before the marriage or civil partnership, so long as it was acquired for use by the parties as a family home or as furniture or plenishings for such a home.

The definition is to be applied quite literally, with the result that property that is not originally matrimonial property can become matrimonial property if it has changed its nature in some way. For example, a partner to a marriage or civil partnership may inherit some money during the marriage or civil partnership. That money, as inherited property, cannot be matrimonial or partnership property notwithstanding that it was acquired during the marriage or civil partnership (since inherited property is excluded from the definition in s 10(4)). But if the partner uses that money to buy something, such as a house or a car, then the house or car has been acquired during the marriage or civil partnership, it has not been (itself) inherited, and therefore it is "matrimonial property" and available for distribution under the Principle in s 9(1)(a). Even something as simple as moving money from one institutional depository to another may have the effect of changing it from non-matrimonial to matrimonial property.

FAIR SHARING OF MATRIMONIAL PROPERTY: FAIR SHARING

The s 9(1)(a) Principle requires that the net value of the matrimonial property be shared "fairly" between the parties. There is a presumption that fair sharing means equal sharing, with the result that the parties can expect to take away from the marriage or civil partnership 50 per cent of the matrimonial property, irrespective of who, before the divorce, dissolution or annulment, actually owned the property. This equal split of the matrimonial property does not require the court to award half of every item to each party. Rather, the court is seeking a universal figure of the matrimonial property, which is then notionally divided by two to give the figure that each can expect to take. If their ownership of matrimonial property is 50–50 in any case then s 9(1)(a) does not justify any award of financial provision (unless s 10(6), discussed below, applies). If, as will be the usual case, there is a disparity in the share each owns of the matrimonial property, then the Principle justifies the court making an order to transfer half the difference, either in cash or in property. For example, imagine a couple jointly own the family home worth £100,000, each has a car (A owns a car worth £5,000 and B owns a car worth £2,000) and A has shares worth £15,000 (their other property not coming within the definition of matrimonial property). Here, the total matrimonial property is £122,000 and so each can expect to take £61,000 away. Since A already owns £70,000 (half the house, her car and the shares) and B already owns £52,000 (half the house and the other car), a transfer from A to B of £9,000 is required to ensure that each leaves the marriage with the correct amount of £61,000. How A pays this to her ex-wife is a matter for negotiation but if the parties cannot agree the court will decide and can require A either to make a cash settlement or to transfer an item of property worth £9,000.

One final point to note in relation to the Principle in s 9(1)(a) is that the statute seeks to achieve a "fair" share rather than an "equal" share. It follows that while equality is presumed to be fair, this presumption can be overturned. So a party can argue that he or she should receive more than a half or that the other should receive less than a half, on the basis that there are special circumstances justifying this departure from equal sharing. Section 10(6) lists examples of what amounts to special circumstances and includes things like any agreement between the parties as to the division of the matrimonial property, the sources of the funds used to acquire the matrimonial property, any dissipation by one party of matrimonial funds and the nature of the property, including whether it is used for the business purposes of one of the parties.

THE OTHER SECTION 9 PRINCIPLES

There are four other Principles in s 9(1) of the Family Law (Scotland) Act 1985, each of which may be used to justify a claim for financial provision on divorce, dissolution or annulment of a marriage or civil partnership.

Principle 9(1)(b) provides that fair account should be taken of any economic advantage derived by either party from contributions, whether financial or otherwise, of the other; and of any economic disadvantages suffered by either party in the interests of the other party or of the family. A partner who gives up a job for the sake of the family (typically, when a woman gives birth and takes time out of her career) suffers an economic disadvantage vis-à-vis her partner who is able to continue working and improving his or her career, and this principle is designed to recognise this and allow the court to make such financial provision as will equalise the partners. As with fair sharing of matrimonial property, this principle only justifies a one-off payment of either cash or property, and in determining the appropriate amount the court is able to take account of the extent to which the economic advantages and disadvantages have been evened out by an award justified by the fair sharing of matrimonial property.

Principle 9(1)(c) provides that any economic burden of caring for a child of the family under the age of 16 years should be shared fairly between the parties. The economic burden is the actual costs of bringing up a child and not the minimal obligation of reasonable aliment that an absent parent owes to the child in any case. The residence parent invariably spends substantially more than is absolutely necessary to provide the child with food, shelter and clothing, and this principle justifies the court making an award to the residence parent to ensure that this actual expenditure is shared fairly with the non-resident parent. Frequently it is satisfied by the court transferring to the parent with residence of the child the half share of the family home that belonged, before divorce, dissolution or annulment, to the non-resident parent: this has the added attraction of ensuring that the children are able to continue residing in the home that they are used to. This Principle can justify the court making a periodical allowance as well as a transfer of property, which is sometimes appropriate since child-rearing expenses are ongoing and often unpredictable. However, if a periodical allowance is made, it comes to an end on the child's 16th birthday and so it is not indefinite.

Principle 9(1)(d) provides that a party who has been dependent to a substantial degree on the financial support of the other party should be awarded such financial provision as is reasonable to enable him or her to adjust, over a period of not more than three years from the date of the decree, to the loss of that support by the divorce, dissolution or annulment. This is designed to provide a three-year cushion to persons who have been long out of the job market and would, therefore, require some retraining before being able to become fully independent. The court will have regard to such matters as the age, health and earning capacity of the party claiming financial provision justified by this Principle, the duration and extent of the claimant's financial dependency and any intention of the claimant to undergo training. Another matter which the court is able to take into account is the conduct of either party, but only if it would be inequitable to leave it out of account. Generally conduct is irrelevant (unless it affects the resources available for distribution) and the court will not take it into account in determining any of the preceding Principles. Either a one-off payment or a periodical allowance may be made here, but if the latter only for three years.

Finally, the principle in s 9(1)(e) provides that a party who at the time of the divorce, dissolution or annulment seems likely to suffer serious financial hardship as a result of the divorce should be awarded such financial provision as is reasonable to relieve him or her of hardship over a reasonable period of time. This is a "safety net" provision designed to ensure that a party on divorce or dissolution does not suffer serious financial hardship which cannot be resolved by any of the other Principles. There may, for example, be very little in the way of matrimonial property and in that situation if one partner is a high earner and the other not, the other may claim that he or she would suffer serious financial hardship by losing the right to claim aliment, or a share of the other's pension, or later succession rights. Though a one-off payment may be made, it is more common for a periodical allowance to be awarded under this Principle and, if so, this is the only Principle that justifies an indefinite periodical allowance. Doing so goes against the main thrust of the 1985 Act, which is to encourage a "clean break" between the parties. In determining what award to make under this principle, the court may have regard to the age, health and earning capacity of the party claiming financial provision, the standard of living of the parties during the marriage or civil partnership, the needs and resources of the parties and also (as with the principle in s 9(1)(d) but none of the others) the conduct of the parties if it would be manifestly inequitable to leave that conduct out of account.

MARITAL AGREEMENTS

The rules discussed above are default rules in the sense that they apply in the absence of any agreement to the contrary. It is open to the parties to agree, either before the marriage or civil partnership, or during it, or on separation, or before divorce or dissolution, a scheme of division that suits themselves better than what the 1985 Act would provide. Such an agreement is enforceable in Scots law, notwithstanding that the effect is to oust the jurisdiction of the court to make financial provision under sections 8 and 9 as discussed above. The only parts of any such agreement that would not be enforced are those dealing with children (where the principles in the Children (Scotland) Act 1995 apply irrespective of the parties' agreement to the contrary) and any provision purporting to limit the right to seek a divorce or dissolution in the first place.

A marital agreement entered into by marriage partners or civil partners may, however, be set aside or varied by the court under s 16 of the Family Law (Scotland) Act 1985. The ground for doing so is that the agreement has been shown to be not fair and reasonable at the time it was made. The agreement may be challenged as being either "unfair" or "unreasonable". Fairness refers to the circumstances in which the agreement was reached while reasonableness refers to its effects. Deliberately withholding information, or undue pressure on a spouse to sign an agreement, or agreeing in the absence of independent legal advice, may all be unfair. A gross disparity in the outcome might be unreasonable (though simply making a bad bargain is not).

An agreement made by a cohabiting couple as to what financial arrangements will be made if they separate is equally enforceable, but there is no means of setting it aside on the basis that it is unfair or unreasonable. Spouses and civil partners have, as usual, greater legal protection than cohabitants.

Essential Facts

- Financial provision on divorce, dissolution or annulment aims to achieve a "clean break" by preferring a one-off payment from one to the other: this way independence is encouraged.

- It does not matter for the purposes of financial provision on divorce/dissolution who is the pursuer in the divorce and who the defender: either may make a financial claim against the other. Conduct of the parties is to be left entirely out of account, unless the conduct adversely affects the resources available for distribution or, in the case of claims under s 9(1)(d) or (e), it would be manifestly inequitable to leave the conduct out of account.

- On divorce, dissolution or annulment, a claim to 50 per cent of the property acquired during the marriage or civil partnership (called the "matrimonial property" or "partnership property") is virtually a claim of right.

- The matrimonial property is valued at the "relevant date" which is (basically) the date of final separation.

- The 50–50 split of matrimonial property is merely presumed to be fair and either party has the opportunity to justify a different division by proving the existence of special circumstances.

- A claim for financial provision under s 9(1)(b) requires there to have been an imbalance in the contributions made or disadvantages suffered for the good of the relationship.

- A claim for financial provision under s 9(1)(c) may allow actual childcare costs to be shared by capital sum, or by way of periodical allowance until the child is 16.

- A claim for financial provision under s 9(1)(d) gives a three-year cushion to allow the claimant to adjust to the loss of spousal support.

- A claim for financial provision under s 9(1)(e) is a safety net against serious financial hardship caused by the divorce or dissolution or annulment. "Caused" is the important word in that sentence.

Essential Statutes

Family Law (Scotland) Act 1985

Section 8(1) sets out the orders that might be made by a court on dissolving a marriage or civil partnership. Section 8(2) provides that any such order must be both justified by one of more of the s 9 Principles and also be reasonable having regard to the resources of the parties. Section 9(1) sets out the five principles that justify an order under s 8. Section 10(1) provides that fair sharing of matrimonial property for the purposes of s 9(1)(a) is presumed to be equal sharing. Section 10(4) defines "matrimonial property" for the purposes of s 9(1)(a). Section 10(6) provides examples of circumstances in which a fair sharing of matrimonial property can be otherwise than an equal sharing. Section 11 sets out the factors that may be taken into account in assessing claims under s 9(1)(b), (c), (d) and (e). Section 13 provides that an award of a periodical allowance may not be made except in a claim under s 9(1)(c), (d) or (e) and in any case may only be made if the court is satisfied that an order for payment of a capital sum, or a transfer of property, or a pension sharing order would be inappropriate or insufficient to satisfy the requirements of s 8(2). Section 16 allows the court to set aside an agreement made by the parties to a marriage/civil partnership as to the financial provision that is to be made on divorce/dissolution on the ground that the agreement was not fair and reasonable at the time it was entered into.

Essential Cases

Skarpaas v Skarpaas (1991): a s 9(1)(a) claim. Dorothy Skarpaas sued her husband, Torsteinn Skarpaas, for divorce and she sought financial provision from him. His only asset was an amount of money he had obtained as damages after an accident at work. The damages had been paid after the relevant date, but the accident was suffered during the marriage and before the relevant date. Mr Skarpaas claimed that the money, having been obtained after the relevant date, was not matrimonial property; and that in any case since it was damages for a personal injury suffered by him the sharing of that asset should not be 50–50 but 100 per cent to him.

The court held that the damages were "matrimonial property" because the right to obtain damages had arisen before the relevant date; that while some departure from a 50–50 split was justified in relation to the portion of the damages referable to solatium, the major portion was for loss of earnings which should be shared 50–50. So Mrs Skarpaas was entitled to a share in the damages, though not as much as 50 per cent. However, Mr Skarpaas had taken to drink after the accident, reducing the total assets available for distribution, and so the sheriff held that, taking this into account, Mrs Skarpaas's claim should be brought back up to 50 per cent of the total remaining matrimonial property.

Davidson v Davidson (1994): a s 9(1)(a) claim. Anna Davidson sued her husband, James Davidson, for divorce. At the relevant date, Mrs Davidson owned investments of almost half a million pounds, but this was not matrimonial property. During the marriage Mr and Mrs Davidson purchased a farm, which Mrs Davidson worked. This was the sole item of matrimonial property. Mrs Davidson continued to look after the children and work the farm; Mr Davidson's timber business had failed and he had fallen into ill health which meant he could no longer work. He sought financial provision: a half share of the farm.

The court held that since the farm had been purchased with money inherited by Mrs Davidson it would be wrong to give Mr Davidson his full claim of one half. But given his impoverished state in comparison to his ex-wife, he ought to receive part of the matrimonial property and an order was made for Mrs Davidson to pay over to her ex-husband an amount representing around one third of the value of the farm.

Whittome v Whittome (No 1) (1994): a s 9 (1)(a) claim. Timothy Whittome sued his wife, Beverly Whittome, for divorce and Beverly claimed a half share of the matrimonial property. The issue was whether a shareholding belonging to Timothy was matrimonial property and required to be part of the calculation. The shares were in a private family company (Christian Salvesen) and Timothy had acquired them over the years partly as a gift from his uncle (Mr Norman Salvesen) and partly as payments from various trust funds set up by the Salvesen family. Beverly argued that the company had undergone various reconstitutions and so the original shares that Timothy had acquired by gift and succession were not the shares he now held: rather, he had acquired the current shares directly from the company.

The court held that the shares held by Timothy, issued by the company, were the shares he originally acquired by gift or succession; that the company reconstitutions did not affect this conclusion; and that therefore the shares were not "matrimonial property" to which Beverly had a claim. (It was also held that an increase in the value of non-matrimonial property during the marriage is not in itself matrimonial property.)

Cunniff v Cunniff (1999): a s 9(1)(a) claim. Dorothy Cunniff sued her husband, Kevin Cunniff, for divorce and sought financial provision. Kevin's financial affairs were complex but he was a high earner and was adept at avoiding his liabilities (such as a tax liability to the Irish Government). Between the date of separation (the relevant date) and the date of the court action for divorce, Kevin had transferred most of his realisable assets into his pension fund, and at the date of proof the only substantial piece of matrimonial property left was the matrimonial home in which Mrs Cunniff and the youngest child of the marriage continued to live. The house was owned jointly and the financial provision ordered by the Lord Ordinary was to require Mr Cunniff to transfer his half share of the house to his ex-wife. He appealed on the ground that this amounted to Mrs Cunniff receiving virtually 100% of the matrimonial property and to a requirement that he transfer all his realisable property to her.

The Inner House held that the decision of the Lord Ordinary was justified. Mr Cunniff had a valuable pension which was part of the "resources" that the court could take into account in determining whether the outcome was reasonable or not. Transferring all the matrimonial assets from one to the other was also reasonable because Mr Cunniff remained in a high earning position and could easily look after himself even if he ended the marriage with no assets; Mrs Cunniff on the other hand (having been out of the job market for many years) could not so readily earn an income and she had continuing obligations to look after the child.

Sweeney v Sweeney (2004): a s 9(1)(a) claim. Susan Sweeney sued Patrick Sweeney for divorce and sought a share in the extensive matrimonial property owned by her husband. The Lord Ordinary valued the property under deduction of capital gains tax, since Mr Sweeney would have to sell the property to meet Mrs Sweeney's claims and he would be liable to that tax charge. On appeal the Inner House held that the value of the matrimonial property was the value that a purchaser would pay, not the value that a seller would receive, and so the Lord Ordinary had erred in deducting capital gains tax before sharing the remainder between the parties.

Mr Sweeney then cross appealed on the ground that there were special circumstances justifying him in paying to his ex-wife less than 50 per cent. In particular he argued that his remaining assets were business assets and not easily realised. Mrs Sweeney pointed out that since the original decree Mr Sweeney had been busy transferring assets from a realisable nature to a non-realisable nature (that is to say, putting his free funds into his business).

The Inner House held that Mr Sweeney had not acted unreasonably and that the difficulty in realising his assets was indeed a special circumstance justifying a departure from equal sharing. So Mr Sweeney was ordered to pay rather less than half the value of the matrimonial property.

Maclachlan v Maclachlan (1998): s 9 (1)(a) and (c) claims. Donalda Maclachlan sued her husband, Thomas, for divorce. The children were to stay with her. The main asset was the matrimonial home, which was jointly owned, but there were other items of matrimonial property and Donalda owned more than Thomas. Both Donalda and Thomas sought financial provision from the other: he sought 50 per cent of the other items of matrimonial property (s 9(1)(a)); she sought a capital sum to help her purchase a house for herself and the children and to help her pay the children's school fees (s 9(1)(c)).

The court held that it was not appropriate to make an award of a capital sum to cover revenue expenses such as school fees, so that claim was dismissed. Thomas's claim to a share of the matrimonial property was valid; so was Donalda's claim for a share of the costs of bringing up the children. But the value of each claim was roughly the same and so cancelled each other out. No order for financial provision was made to either party.

Loudon v Loudon (1994): s 9 (1)(a) and (d) claims. Alison Loudon sued her husband, Gavin Loudon, for divorce. They had been married for seventeen years and Mrs Loudon had not worked since the birth of the child of the marriage. The matrimonial property amounted to £830,000; Mr Loudon was earning around £58,000 per annum net of tax and Mrs Loudon was earning nothing.

The court held that, to reflect Mrs Loudon's contributions to the marriage (looking after the house and the child and relieving Mr Loudon of these responsibilities so that he could advance his own career), she should receive 55 per cent of the matrimonial property; and that in addition she should receive a periodical allowance of £500 a month for two years to allow her to be retrained for the job market.

Haughan v Haughan (2002): a s 9(1)(e) claim. Kathleen Haughan sued her husband for divorce and as financial provision she sought payment of a periodical allowance under s 9(1)(e) of the Family Law (Scotland) Act 1985. This permits a periodical allowance to be ordered if this is necessary to avoid serious financial hardship. Mrs Haughan was 51 years old, had been married for twenty-seven years and during all that time had been dependent on her husband: she was the homemaker and the parties had lived in some comfort. Since the separation she had received no aliment from her husband, was dependent on state benefit and was in poor health: her chances of employment were very low. Mr Haughan, on the other hand, enjoyed good health and earned around £74,000 a year, with an excess of income over expenditure of some £12,000 per year. The Lord Ordinary awarded Mrs Haughan a periodical allowance of £1,000 per month.

Mr Haughan then lost his job and he sought a variation of this award to nil. He had in the interim paid Mrs Haughan nothing. The Inner House held that there had been a change in circumstances but that he could still afford to pay his ex-wife something. A periodical allowance of £500 per month was substituted for the original award.

M v M (2014): s 9(1)(a), (b), (c), (d) and (e) claims. The husband inherited, before the marriage, a landed estate of 1,400 acres comprising a manor house and various tenanted farms. This was not matrimonial property. The wife inherited, during marriage, sums of money which she invested in a farm business attached to her husband's estate. This was matrimonial property. In dividing the matrimonial property the court took account of the source of the funds (the wife's family inheritance) and allowed her 90 per cent. She had given up her career to assist in the running of the estate, in particular organising weekend shooting parties; after separation she would be looking after the children. The court awarded her a lump sum of £250,000 to reflect these contributions under s 9(1)(b) and (c). She was also awarded a periodical allowance for the next three years under s 9(1)(d) and (e) because her earning capacity was restricted while she was bringing up the children (who would all be 18 and in higher education in three years' time) and because serious financial hardship was to be assessed by reference to each claimant's circumstances and not to some objective subsistence provision – in other words, life as a single suburban mother was a serious financial hardship to someone used to being the lady of the manor.

Banks v Banks (2005): Mr and Mrs Banks married in 1965 and, though two children were born of the marriage, Mr Banks took little part in family life. The parties stopped sharing a bedroom in 1988. In 1993, Mr Banks took up a new job overseas and thereafter he seldom spent more than two weeks a year with his family although he continued to support them. In 1994, Mrs Banks and the children visited him for a holiday abroad and she might have shared a hotel room with him. In 1997, Mr Banks moved back to the UK, but not back to the family home; he continued to spend large amounts of time working overseas. In 1998, Mr and Mrs Banks had a meeting to discuss the future financial arrangements between the two of them. They ate their last meal together in 2001. In 2003, Mr Banks informed his wife that he would not be returning to her. They divorced in 2005. The question before the court was: when was the "relevant date" (that is, the date of final separation) which was essential for valuing the matrimonial property for financial provision? The property (most of which was in the name of Mr Banks) had increased in value over the years and so it was in Mrs Banks' interests that the relevant date be as late as possible and in Mr Banks' interests that the relevant date be as early as possible. She argued for 2003 when she was informed that he was not coming back, he for 1993 when he had decided in his own mind that the marriage was effectively dead.

The court held that the separation occurred somewhere in between these two dates and considered that the financial meeting in 1998 was significant as a change in the nature of the relationship between the parties. It held that they had separated from that date and so the date of valuation of the matrimonial property was then.

INDEX